PUTTING LIBRARY INSTRUCTION IN ITS PLACE

LIBRARY ORIENTATION SERIES

PUTTING LIBRARY INSTRUCTION IN ITS PLACE:

IN THE LIBRARY
AND IN THE
LIBRARY SCHOOL

Papers Presented at the Seventh Annual Conference
on Library Orientation for Academic Libraries
held at Eastern Michigan University, May 12-13, 1977

edited by
Carolyn A. Kirkendall

Director, Project LOEX
Center of Educational Resources
Eastern Michigan University

Published for the
Center of Educational Resources,
Eastern Michigan University
by

Pierian Press

ANN ARBOR, MICHIGAN
1978

Library of Congress Catalog Card No. 78-53996
ISBN 0-87650-092-0

PIERIAN PRESS
P.O. Box 1808
Ann Arbor, Michigan 48106

Contents

Preface

Carolyn A. Kirkendall
Director, Project LOEX

The Seventh Annual Conference on Library Orientation for Academic Libraries was held May 12 and 13, 1977, at Eastern Michigan University.

Entitled *Putting Instruction in Its Place: In the Library and in the Library School,* the conference addressed two major themes: obtaining library administrative support, and incorporating instruction into both the library science school curriculum and the continuing education process.

The topic of establishing and implementing courserelated library instruction programs for subject majors was also presented in panel discussion format.

Small group discussions provided the opportunity to informally consider the specifics budgeting and personnel in instruction, faculty contact and involvement, methods and materials, and promoting administrative support for programs. An additional session covered the course work presented in one library school bibliographic instruction course.

Participants were hosted at a cocktail party by Pierian Press. As always, this occasion provided a valuable opportunity for conference participants to learn of the "nuts and bolts" activities of other practicing instruction librarians in an informal setting.

Project LOEX is particularly grateful to the Pierian Press, and to the following individuals who attended and participated in this year's meeting: President James H. Brickley, of Eastern Michigan University, for his enthusiastic and supportive welcome; Floy A. Brown, Program Officer of the College Library Program of the National Endowment for the Humanities; Leone I. Newkirk, Program Associate, and Nancy E. Gwinn, Information and Publications Officer, from the Council on Library Resources.

Appreciation is also extended to those who skillfully participated as group discussion leaders: Anne Beaubien (University of Michigan), Joyce Bennett (Sangamon State University), Joe Boissé (University of Wisconsin--Parkside), Miriam Dudley (University of California at Los Angeles), Hal Espo (Earlham College), Evan Farber (Earlham College), Mary George (University of Michigan), Larry Hardesty (DePauw University), Dwight Hendricks (Eastern Michigan University), Sharon Hogan (University of Michigan), Joan Ormon--droyd (Cornell), Jane Pressau (Presbyterian College), Hugh Pritchard (University of New Hampshire), Sharon Rogers (University of Toledo), Kay Rottsalk (St. Olaf College), Carla Stoffle (University of Wisconsin--Parkside), Cleo Treadway (Tusculum College) and Marvin Wiggins (Brigham Young University).

Special recognition is also extended to all speakers for their comprehensive and thought--provoking presentations, to James E. Mathias, Director of EMU's McKenny Union and to his staff for excellent support services, to Fred Peters and Marian Bevier of the University's Conference Office, to the staff of EMU's Center of Educational Resources, and particularly to the Project LOEX secretary, Patricia McCreery. An expression of thanks is also grate--fully extended to Jo Atchinson, Dwight Hendricks, and Diane Hovatter of the CER Orientation Office for their reliable and in--valuable assistance.

Carolyn A. Kirkendall
September 7, 1977

INTRODUCTION
TO THE CONFERENCE

Fred Blum, Director
Center of Educational Resources
Eastern Michigan University

At the last two conferences, I welcomed the participants with remarks on the history of EMU's Library Orientation Program, an overview of the presentations they would be hearing, and even some observations on getting administrative support for library orientation.

This year I decided that rather than run the risk of repetition, I would limit myself to three things: first, saying "Welcome" on behalf of the Center of Educational Resources; secondly, inviting you to take a few moments from your busy schedule to visit the Center of Educational Resources and to meet the members of our staff who are manning the fort while the rest of us are participating in this program; and finally, thanking Carolyn Kirkendall and Dwight Hendricks for the excellent job they've done in preparing for this conference.

I hope you will find, not only the presentations, but also the arrangements that have been made for wining, dining, and housing you, to your liking.

At this point, then, I should sit down, but before doing so, there are a few things I'd like to add.

As usual, the Conference was a sellout long before May, with over 150 librarians from most states, including Alaska and Hawaii, participating. Seven Canadian provinces and Great Britain are also represented.

It is a particular pleasure to have Nancy Gwinn and Leone Newkirk from the Council on Library Resources, and Floy Brown, who is in charge of College Library Program Grants at the National Endowment for the Humanities, present. The Library Orientation Program at Eastern Michigan University was originally funded by these organizations.

If I were to try to isolate the single most important trend in our Library Orientation Program, I would select the trend towards the application of "Library Use Instruction" to an ever-increasing number of courses and departments. The other side of this coin is the growing involvement of all reference staff in library instruction in their subject fields -- and, as a consequence, the growing involvement of teaching faculty. Thus, the concept of "Library Use Instruction," or should I say *"Better* Library Use Instruction," is having greater impact on larger numbers of students than ever before. Like a peb--ble cast in a stream, the "rippling" effect is impacting total library service.

At the start of this Seventh Conference it is a pleasure to be able to say that library orientation is still a timely topic. Indeed, it is one of the "growth," perhaps I should say "go--go," fields in li--brarianship today. Thus, it is not only a vital area for the profes--sional development of librarians, but also one in which presently there are good career opportunities.

This is reflected in the growing interest library schools are showing in offering courses in library use instruction, as well as the increasing emphasis on this aspect of librarianship in academic libraries.

Hence the theme of this year's conference, which I hope you'll find rewarding, "Putting Instruction in Its Place: In the *Library* and in the Library *School.*"

LIBRARY INSTRUCTION
AND THE ADMINISTRATION

Joseph A. Boissé
Director of the Library/Learning Center
University of Wisconsin—Parkside

In the Bowker volume *Educating the Library User*, edited by John Lubans, Jr., Thomas Kirk did a chapter which he began with two quotations, which I would like to use here, as well.

"The average college student . . . is ignorant of the greater part of the bibliographical apparatus which the skilled librarian has in hourly use, to enable him to answer the thousand queries of the public. A little systematic instruction would so start our student in the right methods, that for the rest of their lives all their work in libraries would be more expeditiously accomplished."

From a contemporary fanatic in bibliographic instruction? Hardly. It is from the Annual Report of the President of Columbia University—in 1883!

The equipment of the library will not be finished until it shall have upon its staff men and women whose entire work shall be, not the care of books, not the cataloging of books, but the giving of instruction concerning their use."

This comment is much more recent than the preceding one. It is from an article by W.R. Harper entitled "The Trend of University & College Education in the United States," which appeared in the North American Review of 1902!

Our movement is not new—it has gained new momentum in re-cent years and is only now beginning to move into its rightful place in the spectrum of activities which occur in an academic library.

The title of my paper as it appears in the printed program, "Library Instruction and the Administration," is vague—purposefully vague, I was told. When I first read the title, I was a little concerned about the breadth of the topic. However, as I reflected on the topic and mulled over the issues and problems which I want to share with you today, I was pleased that the title is, indeed, as general as it is.

I want, first of all, to make quite clear the point of view from which I am speaking. You have before you a library director who is committed to a program of bibliographic instruction. I come from a strong service orientation and, therefore, the professional staff at UW--Parkside did not have to convince me of the value of such a program when I assumed the directorship in September 1973. I am quite convinced that bibliographic instruction is an essential component of a total library program. It is as essential as any of the other functions usually considered an integral part of a library. In fact, it is more essential than many functions considered important in an awfully large number of libraries.

Now then, a topic such as "library instruction and the admini--stration" offers several facets which can be examined. While the problems can be organized in various ways, I have chosen to group them in the following three categories: the problems related to convincing a skeptical library director that bibliographic instruction is a worthwhile activity; the various, and sometimes perhaps insur--mountable, problems that a willing library director will encounter during the development and implementation of such a program; and lastly, the problems associated with convincing the university or col--lege administration that library instruction should be an integral part of the library program.

All the problems encountered in each of these contexts are worth exploring. I could not possibly cover all of the problems which might arise in the allocated time; I am rather going to address some of the more obvious and vexing difficulties which each of us has to deal with to one degree or another.

In the case of the last two groupings of problems, I can speak not only from observation, but, indeed, from personal experience. I will, on the contrary, address the first configuration of problems more from a theoretical point of view, since I have neither had to convince a director myself, nor be convinced as a director that bib--liographic instruction was worthwhile pursuing.

Library staff will find that a non--supportive director will place rather formidable obstacles in their way. The administrator who, in his or her own mind, is not prepared to support the endeavor will re--fuse to allocate resources to the project. The staff position re--quested for bibliographic instruction will never be funded; money will never be available to purchase materials necessary to the imple--mentation of the program. Anne Passarelli and Millicent Abell explained the problem quite clearly:

"Meaningful support of the undergraduate library goals by the library administration must include adequate budget for

2

staff as well as materials. When the undergraduate library staff is reduced to a skeleton level of two or three, the library ad--ministration usually has no expectation that instructional ser--vices are to be offered. Several librarians mention that they have requested a position in their libraries of orientation or instruction librarian without success. If the library administra-tion does not recognize the peculiar capabilities of the under--graduate library, but sees it primarily as a study hall, the li--brary's chances for survival, to say nothing of effectiveness, are greatly reduced." (1

The authors, of course, were addressing themselves to under--graudate libraries at large universities. The situation, however, is not all that different at smaller, primarily undergraduate, institutions. The same kind of commitment of personnel and material by the chief administrator is essential if a bibliographic instruction program is to do anything but flounder and fail.

To my knowledge, no one has undertaken a serious study to isolate and explain the reasons behind the general reluctance, if not outright opposition, on the part of administration, to make this commitment. I would at least like to share with you some thoughts which I have on the subject.

I am convinced, in the first place, that the majority of directors of academic libraries understand neither what bibliographic instruc--tion really is, nor what its rightful place in the library should be. It certainly is not, in their view, an elemental library activity. If it were, the thrust of the last five to ten years in the area of biblio--graphic instruction would not have been the grass roots movement that it was. Library directors, while they may be strange birds in many respects, universally want a good institution providing good services. Given that assumption, and assuring they understood what we are talking about, you would necessarily see bibliographic in--struction enjoying a far more favored position in academic libraries.

While this first reason centered on a lack of knowledge, the next one is connected rather to the kind of individuals from whose ranks directors have been recruited in recent years. In the period of af--fluence which ended with the early years of this decade, emphasis was generally placed on the construction of new libraries and the acquisition of collections to fill the stacks. In many libraries, public services -- and I include biliographic instruction in that area -- was a stepchild. Library reports regularly stressed the growth in the size of collections. Statistics generally emphasized collection growth and circulation, neither of which is an indicator of real service. Quite naturally, directors were appointed who would pay attention to these concerns.

There still exists, on many academic campuses, a feeling that the chief library administrator need not be a person with any kind of experience with or commitment to public service. Strong statement? Agreed, but one which, I think, is borne out by the advertisements which appear for director's position. Look at a sampling from the last several issues of *College and Research Libraries News* or *The Chronicle of Higher Education.* You will find that, in addition to management skills and experience, what is required most frequently is "familiarity with OCLC," "understanding of management systems, automation, and computer facilities," "a solid grasp of management systems, automation and computer applications," "knowledge of current trends in academic libraries, budgeting, operations management," "knowledge of and experience with all phases of library operation including automation applications and in collection development," "demonstrated ability and knowledge of automation, business management and personnel administration." Note that not one of the position announcements to which I referred required, or even asked for, familiarity with the public service aspects of librarianship. That fact is a sad commentary.

Some people would attempt to explain the situation by saying that the commitment to which I refer is obviously understood in these advertisements. If that is the case, why is it necessary to refer specifically to management skills? It seems to me that those skills would just as easily be taken for granted. It is obvious that the individuals responsible for developing position descriptions have an extremely myopic view of the true function of a library.

I have mentioned all of this to support my assertion that the majority of directors are not really concerned about public service or bibliographic instruction. Their orientation is toward buildings and computers. Please don't misunderstand me. I have nothing against these activities. However, they should never become ends in themselves. The building, the collection of materials and the computer are all means to an end and that end is the dissemination of information.

Professional library staff must insist on influencing the recruitment process more than they have in the past. When an academic institution is undertaking the recruitment of a new library director, the staff should be expressing its opinion about what kind of person they feel should be recruited. Communicate with the university administrator, be he a dean or a vice-chancellor, who heads the recruitment process. Do not wait to be asked for your opinion, if you do, you may wait a long time!

The statement I quoted earlier insisted that meaningful support entailed adequate staff and resources. The statement is so simple and seems so obvious that one is tempted to react scornfully. I'm sure that the authors do not make it lightly and wouldn't want it to be treated as such. And I could not agree more with them. If a director, in a period of magnanimity, allocates a sum of money from his special funds, for purchase of materials related to bibliographic instruction without ever putting it in the budget as a line item, the entire undertaking is on shaky ground. What is likely to occur is that the first time the budget becomes tight, this particular sum of money will simply disappear. In other words, you have to convince the administrator that bibliographic instruction should be as important a component of the total library picture as inter--library loan, binding, circulation, cataloging, or any one of the myriad functions performed by the library.

If bibliographic instruction is to receive this kind of support, and if a director is faced with a static budget, only one course of action is possible: a reprioritization of activities must be undertaken. The statement sounds harmless enough, but the task is herculean. As a result, relatively few library administrators are prepared to under-take it. Reprioritizing involves reexamining every activity to which staff and resources are committed, reevaluating them in the light of limited resources, comparing them against new activities clamoring for recognition and making a judgment. If, indeed, every activity, both old and new, cannot be supported, some will have to be omit-ted. The easiest way is to simply not take on new projects. It is not necessarily the best decision, however. Setting new priorities, estab-lishing new goals and objectives is never a simple undertaking. The director will have to face pressure from any number of sources and will have to be prepared to justify decision by rational explanations.

Every administrator must be prepared to do so or that individual is a failure as an administrator.

Support of the university administration is quite as crucial as is support of the library administration. It is a level of support, how-ever, which will probably not be attained unless bibliographic instruction already enjoys the support of the library administration.

Depending on how the university administration views the library, the task of education will be easy or difficult. Unfortunately, most of our university and college administrators have an extremely limited view of the role of the library. For the most part, they suffer from what is commonly known as the mausoleum syndrome. In other words, the library is a sort of sacred place where books are housed. Every campus has one and if it has lots of books, it must be good, but it really does not participate in the vital aspects of academic life. At large universities, the administration may make a dis-tinction between the graduate library and the undergraduate library. The former is seen as a resource for faculty and doctoral students, the precious few who presumably are capable of doing research; the latter is more often than not seen as a study hall for undergraduates.

At smaller institutions, the study hall mentality generally prevails.

If I sound a bit harsh, it's because I am intending to be. But take a moment to think about it. Ask yourself when you last saw your president, chancellor, vice–chancellor or dean in the library; ask yourself how familiar they are with library programs and activities; ask yourself when the last time was that the chief administrative officer referred to the library as more than "an outstanding collection of books and periodicals"; ask yourself when the university officer to whom the director reports last attended a library conference or symposium of some sort. The answers to these questions will tell you a great deal about the kind of support that the library enjoys on your campus. And keep in mind that just as you have to compete for a share of the library's financial pie, the director of the library has to compete for a share of the university pie.

When academic institutions are reevaluating activities because of static or decreasing budgets, the library will come under scrutiny. It is, in fact, particularly vulnerable because that capital budget looms mighty large. In any case, the tendency will be to question new programs, new activities. I have met some administrators and faculty who would cut anything and everything rather than reduce by one volume the acquisition rate. These people obviously have a terminal case of the mausoleum syndrome. In recent years, my own institution has gone through rather severe retrenchment and we have had to justify every library activity. At no time have we considered eliminating our bibliographic instruction activities.

How have we gone about educating the university administration to the value of a well–planned, comprehensive program of bibliographic instruction? In a variety of ways. My role, as director, has been to explain to the administration what we are attempting to do and why. I explain budgetary needs as well as program activities. As we obtain results from our pre–– and post––testing projects, I forward these with commentary to appropriate administrators. I bring to their attention some of the statistics which, we feel, are relevant. For instance, I have emphasized a sharp increase in our circulation in spite of a decline in the enrollment. A constant flow of information runs from my office to that of the Assistant Chancellor, to whom I report.

The Library/Learning staff, on the other hand, have worked with faculty and have developed a strong base of support in that quarter. This support has been built over a period of time. Our strategy for enlisting faculty in our instructional efforts has been patterned on the old saying, "You catch more flies with a teaspoon of honey than a teaspoon of vinegar." We concentrated from the first on individuals who are already library supporters and who expressed an interest in our program of bibliographic instruction.

6

Others soon became interested, lest they miss out on something. In any case, a solid core of faculty supporters gradually developed and the university administration has observed its development. In fact, the administration is quick to observe faculty support for any undertaking.

In the realm of the academic world, every university admini--stration answers to someone or some group. In a system such as the University of Wisconsin, the local Chancellor answers to a Central Administration; in other situations, it may be to a Board of Trustees. In any case, the local administration is anxious to point to success--ful programs. I assure you that a well--planned, carefully imple--mented program of bibliographic instruction cannot fail. It will be a success; students will learn new skills which will improve their per--formance across the curriculum; the university administration will take pride in the project; a strong coalition of library support will be found; and you will be amazed at the results.

Currently, the Library/Learning Center at UW--Parkside enjoys a larger per student appropriation than any other campus in the system. We are in a prominent position when comparisons are made and could be subject to budget reductions. Our local administration, however, is willing to defend this allocation. This willingness to fund the Library/Learning Center at a high level stems, in part at least, from a recognition that we are contributing directly and significantly to the instructional process.

Don't get me wrong. This is not going to occur overnight. It will take time. However, if a library develops realistic goals and ob--jectives and attaches them to an equally realistic timetable, it will happen.

I would now like to devote some time to a commentary on a few of the problems which a director might well encounter as he or she guides a program of bibliographic instruction into existence. All of the problems on which I would like to dwell for a few minutes are staff related and all but one are internal.

Let's look first at the external problems, that of recruiting qualified staff. The situation today is such that this recruitment problem can be a major headache. With the ever increasing interest in bibliographic instruction there has been a dramatic increase in the number of listed vacancies for whom candidates with knowledge of bibliographic instruction are being sought. A member of my staff some time ago surveyed the public services position descriptions ad--vertised in *College and Research Libraries News* for the period May 1975 to May 1976. The results of the survey indicate that 19 out of 35 reference position descriptions listed instruction as a part of the duties.

It is a simple fact that our Library Schools are not equipping their graduates with the knowledge and skills which allow them to compete for these positions. The few library school students with whom I have spoken in recent years simply do not have an under-- standing of what bibliographic instruction is all about, or what kinds of skills are required to be a successful bibliographic librarian.

Most of these students think of bibliographic instruction as teaching the use of the card catalog and the common indexes which readily come to mind. What students really need is an understanding of the philosophical base for bibliographic instruction, a knowledge of the various approaches to the task, experience in designing a pro-- gram through the delineation of clear, precise goals and objectives. In addition, they need instruction in designing and producing ma- terials which will assist them in implementing a program.

A few weeks ago, I spoke to a meeting of a state association of academic librarians. In my presentation I discussed at length the ACRL Guidelines on Bibliographic Instruction and also our program at UW--Parkside. During the question and answer period, someone pointed out that what I was saying was not new, that over the years others have worked in this area. I replied that her observations were true, but that over the years bibliographic instruction had consis-- tently been a stepchild in academic libraries. To stress my point, I followed with the challenge: Select any academic library fifteen years ago and find to what extent resources were committed to bib-- liographic instruction activities.

There is no doubt that library administrators must shoulder a large share of the responsibility for this negligence over the years. However, I feel the library schools must accept at least an equal share of the responsibility. While directors should have been far-- sighted enough to perceive the value of this instruction and assign it its rightful place in their library, library schools should have been turning out graduates who would be advocates of bibliographic in-- struction. Neither of these groups met their responsibility in this area.

At no time has either group faced up to the situation. We all know that the "movement" has been an outstanding example of a grass roots movement. The awakening of interest in bibliographic instruction has come from practicing librarians eager to share their knowledge with students. As recently as one year ago, not one li-- brary school in the country listed in its catalog a regularly scheduled course dedicated to bibliographic instruction. We are only now be-- ginning to see courses being developed but even these are "summer specials" or "minicourses." The situation is deplorable.

And yet, our professional associations have addressed the ques-- tion of bibliographic instruction. New guidelines developed by the ALA Reference and Adult Services Division specify that "A specific plan for the instruction of individuals in the use of information aids is to be developed and coordinated among all types of libraries, in-- formation centers or unit of library activity."[2] The "Standards for College Libraries" approved by the Association of College and Re- search Libraries on July 23, 1975, specify that "Proper service shall include: the provision of continuing instruction to patrons in the effective exploitation of libraries. . ."[3] The American Library As-- sociation and National Education Association in *Standards for School Media Programs* indicate that a good media program includes "Instruction to improve learning through the use of printed and audiovisual resources"[4] and that the professional staff implements the program by "assuming responsibility for providing instruction in the use of the media center and its resources that is correlated with the curriculum and that is educationally sound."[5]

It is interesting now to look at some statements from deans/ directors of library schools. The column edited by Carolyn Kirken-- dall in *The Journal of Academic Librarianship* carried commentaries by four educators in the November 1976 issue. The question to which they responded was: "Do deans of library schools agree on the need for library instruction in the library school curriculum?" In their responses, they referred to bibliographic instruction variously as "an issue," "a concept," "a special type of library service," "a ubiquitous topic." They all said it was important, but not one of them referred to it as central to the function of the library. In that observation lies a major part of our problem: until the educators are convinced of the elemental role of bibliographic instruction, these ad hoc courses will continue for the most part to be afterthoughts.

One of the deans makes an analogy between bibliographic instruction and intellectual freedom and refers to both as "trends and issues in librarianship." Another dean referred to bibliographic instruction as "central to the function of the library" and immedi-- ately went on to group it with a "host of other issues just as hot." Both gentlemen miss the point. Is acquisitions a trend or an issue? Is inter--library loan a trend or an issue? Is circulation a trend or an issue? Of course not. They are basic components of library service. And that is precisely how one should view bibliographic instruction.

In that same column, the statement is made by one individual that "whether a given library school should add such a course to its curriculum depends on local needs, the availability of competent faculty to teach the course and a host of other factors." In the first place, any library school that presumes to prepare graduates for positions in academic libraries must address itself to bibliographic instruction. In the second place, there are innumerable competent individuals who can teach such a course if one is willing to go outside the ranks of the regular library school faculty roster. In the last place, I would like to know what the other factors are!

One last comment before we move on to more problems. There are still library schools that regularly offer a course in the history of libraries. Indeed, I believe that it is required in some institutions. It is my opinion, and I hope that I am not alone in espousing it, that bibliographic instruction deserves attention far more than does the history of libraries.

Recently, a colleague described a situation which is lamentable. He is director of a university library serving a student population of some 9,000 individuals. He has a staff which includes some 20 pro-- fessional librarians. He has budget dollars which he is prepared to allocate to bibliographic instruction activities. He is also prepared to assign staff to that function. Sounds great, doesn't it? Not so, since not one of his staff is interested in becoming involved in bibliographic instruction!

How does one tackle a similar situation? Assuming the re-- sources are available, the director attempts to recruit a new staff member with the necessary skills and demonstrated interest. My friend cannot do that since his authorized positions are all filled. The director can also arbitrarily reassign an existing staff member to that activity. Such a course, in my opinion, would guarantee failure before the program were even undertaken. Without a librarian per-- sonally convinced of the value of bibliographic instruction, and personally committed to the program, all efforts would come to naught. As I see it, my colleague can try to reeducate some of his staff. This can be a long, tedious process. Secondly, he can hope for vacancies to occur -- and soon.

Now, then, I want to address the last type of problem. It is a problem that can undermine the best library and a director can encounter it even when he has an outstanding staff.

Earlier in this paper, we mentioned briefly that certain prob-- lems are more likely to occur during periods of financial drought than at other times. Given the realities of our economic situation, we should all be prepared to deal with these problems for the fore-- seeable future. We saw earlier that a commitment to bibliographic instruction necessarily entails an allocation of resources to support the program. In a period of no--growth budgets, this will mean reallocation of existing resources. Bluntly put, administrators will have to rob Peter to pay Paul.

There is no way that we can avoid this dilemma. We are de-- luding ourselves if we act on the premise that large, untapped sources of money are soon to be made available to us. Every single indicator points to the folly of such a belief. Administrators have but one road open to them: they must reexamine existing activities, re-- prioritize programs, and reallocate resources. In the process of reprioritization, not everyone will be pleased. About the only statement upon which we here might all agree is that none of us has enough budget to do everything that we feel our libraries should be doing. Think of what reprioritizing and reallocating may entail. It may mean one less cataloger, or only a part--time special collec--tions librarian. It may mean fewer journal subscriptions or a reduc--tion of our acquisition rate by one thousand volumes.

Now, think for a moment of staff reactions to these alterna--tives. The individuals responsible for each of these areas are not going to weakly surrender funds. They are going to protest; they should protest. As a director, I expect each of my division heads to see his/her area as the most crucial to the successful operation of the library. Only the director is required to have a catholic view of the institution. Therefore, there will be personal jealousies and personal rivalries which will be fanned by this process.

In terms of librarian/teaching faculty relationshiops a further complication arises. As the bibliographic instruction program devel--ops, new contacts between the librarians and other faculty will be generated. The other faculty will become aware of the activities carried on by the instruction librarians and will then begin to ask questions, such as: What do the other librarians do? This is not the sort of question that calms fears and strengthens friendships!

Another related issue which may seem trivial to some, but which is nonetheless real and which can contribute to a general decline in morale, is the following: The instruction librarian is more apt to be involved in social activities of other faculty and this can also set off jealousies. Don't be too quick to laugh and observe that I am referring to pettiness and/or insecurity. I am, but these are feelings with which the director has to deal in one way or another.

All of the foregoing are very real problems which must be solved, they are obstacles which must be overcome. They make the challenge of bibliographic instruction more interesting and the ac--complishments more rewarding.

Some of you may feel that I have been quite negative. Let me assure you that I have not intended to project that attitude. On the contrary, I personally am quite optimistic about the future. The bibliographic instruction movement will not shrivel up and disappear. It is neither a fad, nor a trend. It represents a reawakening on the part of librarians that we are more than acquirers, catalogers and keepers of information; we are teachers and those skills which we can teach are just as important to the overall intellectual life of an academic institution as the knowledge imparted by other faculty members.

Footnotes

1. Passarelli, Anne B. and Abell, Millicent D. "Programs of Under--graduate Libraries and Problems in Educating Library Users" in *Educating the Library User*, ed. by John Lubans, Jr. (New York: Bowker, 1974)
2. American Library Association. Reference and Adult Services Division. *A Commitment to Information Services: Developmental Guidelines.* 1976, p. 3 Mimeo.
3. "Standards for College Libraries." *College and Research Libraries News.* no. 9 (October, 1975) p. 292.
4. American Library Association and National Education Association. *Standards for School Media Programs.* Chicago, 1969, p. 4.
5. Ibid. p. 8.

THE SANGAMON STATE EXPERIENCE

Joyce A. Bennett
Instructional Services Librarian
Sangamon State University Library

In order to experience Sangamon State University Library, you should first meet Sangamon State University. Located in the state capital, Springfield, Illinois, Sangamon State University is a new institution, having open its doors in 1970, after having been established by the Illinois General Assembly in 1969 as the first of two senior institutions in the state. As a senior institution, we have 3600 juniors, seniors, and graduate students – no freshmen and sophomores. This of course has implications for our instructional program, as we have no freshman orientation courses.

Sangamon State was designated as the state's public affairs university, charged with training persons for public service and fostering an active understanding of contemporary social, environmental, technological, and ethical problems as they relate to public policy.

Mandated to be a capstone to the community college system in Illinois, SSU is a commuter institution where every faculty member has a commitment to the individual student, with teaching as the first priority and research and publication serving as support for teaching rather than the opposite. All of Sangamon State's programs are designed in an innovative way, bringing together the world of practical affairs and the world of higher education.

Departments are called programs at SSU and program committees are interdisciplinary. For example, one of our programs is Environments and People. Faculty on the Environments and People program committee may be composed of a scientist, sociologist, historian, as well as a librarian. Our nine librarians have full faculty status and can be full voting members of the programs they work with, participating in personnel decisions and curriculum decision, if they so choose.

The Norris L. Brookens Library opened in January 1976 as the University's first permanent building and emphasizing the University's commitment to its library. The Library's multimedia

13

collection is particularly strong in the social sciences and supports the public affairs mandate of the university. It contains more than 190,000 volumes, 3,100 subscriptions to newspapers and journals, 52,000 government publications, a variety of musical and spoken recordings, simulation games, audio and video tapes, slides, and microform collections. The Library supplements its holdings by cooperative arrangements with other libraries. Tape recorders, filmstrip readers, portable microform readers, and other media equipment are also available to the SSU community. In addition, the Library provides graphic, audio, video, and photographic services for individual students, faculty, and classroom operations.

The SSU Library is an integral component of the instructional process at the university. Based on the concept of the teaching library, students are assisted in acquiring bibliographic knowledge which permits independent and competent use of library resources, not only for the student's brief span of time at SSU but for a lifelong use of all forms of recorded knowledge and experience. Instruction in the library takes place at our reference desk, which we call the Get Help Here desk, through workshops, through team teaching, through tutorials, through formal advance bibliography courses. Each new faculty member who comes to SSU must sign what we call the Blue Memo. Mentioned in this memo is that library literacy is a primary instructional commitment of each professor. We teach not only students, but graduate assistants, secretaries, members of the Springfield community, high school librarians and our own library civil service staff.

Today I have brought with me a slide presentation outlining our basic management style and how it supports our teaching library. I think it is important to point out that we realize we have a more ideal situation than others in terms of institutional budget support and staffing. However, I would like for each of you to work past that fact in order to avoid the pitfall of discounting everything I share with you today as too different to apply to your situation. Rather, I would like for you to consider the Sangamon State exper--ience for what you can appropriate for your own instructional program.

None of us believes that the success of our program depends on a consultative form of management and that everyone should adopt this system in order to implement a library instructional program. What we do believe is that it is important to have as many people as involved as possible in the instructional program. Each Instructional Services Librarian works at the Get Help Here desk, and we advocate this kind of integration, as opposed to a separate instructional team and a separate reference department. Using professional administrators to head all but the reference departments of our library enables the librarians to incorporate Get Help Here desk instruction into the rest of the library's instructional program.

In the past year we have been clarifying our management style, as we work out our relationships with our new Dean of Library Services, Dr. Patricia Breivik, who came to us from Pratt Institute in Brooklyn, New York. It has been a learning experience for all of us and has proved to us that the Sangamon State experience is not dependent on its founders.

On behalf of my colleagues in the SSU library, I want to take this opportunity to thank you for your interest in our library and hope that you will find this presentation enlightening. During the course of this discussion, I will cover five areas that I think may interest you: the decision–making structure of the library, which is based on committees; an explanation of how this structure relates to our teaching philosophy; the rationale for using non–librarians as administrators; reasons for considering our teaching library philosophy; and the role of the Instructional Services Librarian or ISL.

The SSU library, as some of you may know, does not employ librarians as administrators. Instead, all librarians are actively involved in teaching activities. The administrative responsibilities for the departments Media, Circulation, and the technical services (including documents, serials, acquisitions, cataloging and processing) and for Archives are performed by professional, non–librarian administrators.

How does a library start down the road we are on? For us, that journey began seven years ago with the establishment of a new upper division university mandated to be innovative, among other things. The president, Dr. Robert Spencer, believed in the value of library literacy. To accomplish these goals, he sought a librarian who espoused the same beliefs. From behind the ivy covered walls of Harvard, he drew Howard Dillon. Howard also believed in a different role for librarians: "The role in which I see librarians as members of the faculty at Sangamon is as colleagues in the creation of learning environments for students. I see library faculty not as managers of a staff but as teachers of independent problem solving through the use of learning resources in print and other forms of communication. Library faculty assume responsibilities in four specific areas: Each serves students as a reference librarian and each offers workshops on the scope and organization of information in selected areas of study. Secondly, each assumes responsibility for the development of some aspect of our collections, print and non–print. Third, each participates in the decision we must make concerning the way our library organizes and indexes the information we have. The fourth area we call library liaison. Here we move into the classroom situation in a partnership role with another faculty member."

In order to explain how we have undertaken the approaches that we have, let me discuss briefly the management structure of the library.

The library has adopted a form of management in which the Dean, Department Administrators, Head of Archives, ISL's, and elected staff and student representatives share in the decision making process. To accomplish this feat in an orderly fashion, the administrative organization is divided into four committees: Library Administrative Council, Library Cabinet, Library Program Committee and the Faculty Senate Library Committee.

The Administrative Council is responsible for making operational decisions which support established policies and procedures. In this committee the department administrators and Head of Archives meet with the Dean and the Dean's staff to resolve library operational concerns that do not change policy -- such things as internal staffing changes and budget adjustments.

Library goals and operational policy are determined by the Library Cabinet. This committee is comprised of the ISL's, administrators, student representatives, civil service representatives, the Dean and the Administrative Assistants to the Dean. It meets regularly to consider proposals for policy changes and to discuss solutions to procedural problems. The Library Cabinet is also responsible for developing long range plans including budget, staff and space allocations.

The Library Program Committee has the responsibility for the instructional program and library faculty personnel recommendations. Collection development, reference service, bibliographic instruction and liaison relationships with University programs are under its purview. The membership of the Library Program Committee differs from the two previous library committees in that faculty and students from other academic programs are members. This is in keeping with the mandates of the university that require all programs, or departments, to be interdisciplinary. Likewise, our librarians are members of and library liaison to other academic programs such as the Sociology/Anthropology Program Committee and the Communications Program Committee to name but two.

The fourth group, the Faculty Senate Library Committee is a standing committee of the university governance system. This committee, comprised of faculty and students from other academic programs, and the Dean of the library and one ISL as *ex officio*, non-voting, members, was appointed to act as a link between the library and the University community regarding policy or procedural matters. Through information gathered from the University, the Senate committee advises and supports the Library in resolving library issues.

To summarize quickly, the four management groups are:

The Administrative Council, which meets to oversee daily operational matters; the Library Cabinet which sets goals and objectives and determines the operational policy; the Library Program Committee which sets goals, objectives and policy concerning the educational function of the Library, and the Faculty Senate Library Committee which supports and advises the Library on policy questions that affect the University community. As you can tell, the structure of the library is based on a participatory style of management. We find that this style compliments our teaching philosophy by adding an additional degree of responsibility and colleagiality among the Library's teaching faculty and administrative and support staff.

This is not to say that participatory management is without problems. We have our share. As you may have noticed, all major decisions are made by one of the committees, and we all know the result of the committee that set out to construct a horse! The same problems apply for our management structure. There is time lost, a lot of energy burned, and sometimes little mileage. There is also the problem of clearly defining the jurisdiction of each committee *vis à vis* each other and *vis à vis* the Dean. However, we find these problems are solvable in most cases. By forming task forces to work on proposals, establishing an agenda committee to better organize meeting time, compiling written policy statements and standardizing the lines of communication, we have been able to offset many of the drawbacks of the committee process.

The third point that I referred to in the introduction was an explanation of our use of professional administrators rather than librarians to direct the operations of the Media, Circulation and Technical Services departments and Archives. We are often asked by people who visit our library if it is possible for our teaching program to exist and still retain librarians as administrators. The answer is a definite yes – and no. Yes, it is possible but the disadvantages far outweigh the advantages. First, the pros for using professional administrators.

Traditionally librarians in charge of departments have two responsibilities: one, to manage, and two, to provide professional leadership in their particular area of expertise. At SSU we hire a professional administrator to manage the department, and thus gain the advantage of having a specialist in management, thereby freeing the librarian to work as a specialist in librarianship. This allows the librarian and administrator to concentrate on his/her area of expertise. The librarians can devote more time to teaching activities because less time is spent on routine management.

On the other side of the coin are the disadvantages. The major drawback is the on--going need for some professional leadership especially for long--range planning. To meet this need, we have created the role of internal library liaison. Each library administrative department and unit can turn to an ISL who has had previous training and experience in the operation of a similar department or unit. When the administrators need advice on a problem, he/she seeks out the department's liaison. It is important to understand that there is no administrative authority on the part of the librarians in this relationship. The administrator is free to seek advice and follow or ignore it. If a disagreement should arise, the matter would be resolved by the Library Cabinet or the Dean.

This concludes our brief discussion regarding the management structure and how it relates to our teaching philosophy as well as the rationale for using professional administrators as department administrators. Now let's turn our attention to the remaining two points: the benefits of our teaching philosophy and a short description of some of the roles in which our librarians are involved.

There are three benefits derived from Sangamon State's approach to library instruction. The positive effects on the patrons, the effects on the library faculty, and the institutional gains. The patrons who participate in the library instructional process receive training in locating materials and becoming independent users of the library. This we commonly refer to as "library literacy." This training will enable the patron to participate in a self--directed approach to learning as well as become a life--long learner who can utilize information handling skills.

The influences of the program on the library faculty are different for each individual. For some, there is the aspect of being accepted as a faculty colleague by classroom faculty. Another is the colleagiality of working with a group toward mutually acceptable goals. Also, there are the daily learning experiences that come from working with other library faculty who are more experienced in the literature of a specific field than you are. For some, it may be the professional growth that comes from interaction with colleagues in the office, on campus, and at association meetings as well as many other benefits.

The third benefit derived from the library's philosophy is the gains made by the institution. Through formal and informal means of inquiry, we have found that the quality of the library instruction and resources are often responsible for persuading both faculty and students to select SSU. Besides recruiting, the institution is concerned with accreditation and academic reputation. This is an area in which the Library has been effective. During the accreditation process, the Library was cited by the NCA committee as one of the institutions's major accomplishments. In another report for the NCA self study, Dr. David Kaser, Professor of Library Science in the Graduate Library School of Indiana University, noted, ". . . of the many laudable innovations in the SSU community, those in its library structure and service may well be of greatest consequence to society."

Some of you may be thinking that all these things are easy to say, but how do you go about proving their validity? Tough question. Dr. Kaser spoke to this when he said: "It must be pointed out that techniques for evaluating library programs everywhere are notoriously deficient, so that the SSU library will be experimenting even in the preparation of the evaluation research design." Thus, even though many of the evaluations of our library are subjective, we are striving to construct objective means for measuring the results of our teaching.

A few methods used thus far include the use of student evaluations of library faculty, peer evaluations, evaluations from classroom faculty with whom the librarians have worked, questionnaires distributed to the university community and library skills pre-tests and post-tests constructed to measure the degree of learning resulting from one of our methods of instruction. The results gathered through these more objective means of measurement have been very supportive.

There are also a number of subjective indicators. One is the degree of continued commitment from the university administration. At SSU, the library has maintained its share of the total university budget at approximately 11%. Compared to most institutions, this is much higher than average. The financial support as well as the recent upgrading of the Head librarian's position to the level of Dean indicates the support by the administration of our goals. This attitude is well founded according to the two studies mentioned earlier. To quote the NCA team, "The library must definitely be counted as one of the institution's strengths."

Another factor that indicates the influence of our teaching philosophy can be seen in the graduates who have left the University. These students through demands on their local libraries and through the alumni association have attempted to increase the quality of library services available to them in the libraries they go on to use.

Lastly, and somewhat immodestly, we can cite many other institutions who are attempting to implement a teaching service similar to the one at SSU.

Hopefully, by now some of you are considering the merits of our program and are interested in the specific role that the librarians play. I have touched on a number of these points thus far and a complete description of the instructional process would take another complete presentation. However, to conclude this discussion, I will identify some of the key elements.

The ISL's fill out individual workload plans each semester. This is the means by which they identify the amount of time they will commit to service to the University, to the Library, and to teaching. Service to the University may be as a member of the governance system or membership on a standing committee or participation in ad hoc committees or service in one of the University's Public Affairs Centers. Service to the Library will entail work on commit- tees and task forces, special projects, liaisons and collection develop- ment.

Teaching is the third area. Each ISL may commit his/her time in a number of areas. These include: Get Help Here desk instruc- tion, workshops, tutorials, team teaching, or formal semester--long instruction in a field of expertise.

This concludes the discussion of the SSU Library. We have tried to provide a clear picture of our management structure, includ- ing a description of our participatory style of management and use of non--librarian administrators. We also briefly described the teach- ing philosophy of the Library and how the management structure is related to our philosophy. One last point should be made. That is, although our Library has integrated all of these ideas into one system, we feel that the concepts are sound and could stand in- dividually. Thus one library may adopt the teaching library ap- proach and reject the notion of participatory management while another may adopt the use of professional administrators. You might further investigate the ideas we have presented today in the context of your individual circumstances and consider those which would seem most likely to lead to better educated library users.

I have brought with me several items related to our instruction- al program and our management system, which I though would be of interest to you. Included are:

1. Free copies of two documents we recently completed:
   a. SSU Library Management System
   b. Lines of Communication for Effecting Change

2. Revised Instructional Services Librarian Job Description

3. Copy of our workload plan and a completed one with an attached self--evaluation

4. Guidelines and Processes for Library Faculty Evaluation

5. SSU Library Department Administrator General Job De- scription

6.   Reprint of Howard Dillon's article which appeared in the September 1975 issue of *The Journal of Academic Librar-- ianship*

7.   Statements in public relations publications about the Li-- brary in:
     a. Course schedule
     b. College catalog

8.   Copy of our Library Skills Test which we have on PLATO

9.   Course description for two courses we have offered:
     a. Basic Sources of Information
     b. Basic Legal Bibliography

10. A Survey of Library Services at SSU – administered Spring 1977

11. Several documents related to library instructional goals and objectives

12. Sample Guides to Sources, Guides to Services, and Guide to Collections we have authored

13. David Kaser's Report

14. Workshop report form

I know some of you have specific questions regarding the management system, commitment of present administration to in-- struction, evaluating our instructional program and others. So at this time I would like to open the floor for questions.

LIBRARIANS WANT NO WASTED MINDS

A.P. Marshall, Librarian
Center of Educational Resources
Eastern Michigan University

Library science is at long last on the verge of becoming a pro-- fession in the true sense. Perhaps there are a few persons around who questions the validity of this statement, based upon earlier definitions of the word "profession." But in recent years we have slowly been developing a distinct body of knowledge reflecting not only our professional concerns, but also providing guidelines for the provision of a service no one else is prepared to give. Perhaps you are aware of Abraham Flexner's contention in 1915 that a profes- sion had to exhibit a number of distinctive qualities! It was an all or none proposition, so failure of one quality meant that they would fail to meet the qualifications.

First, the specified occupation had to draw upon a store of knowledge that was more than ordinarily complex. This excluded persons with routine and simple skills, those whose competencies were accessible to any native wit, could never properly be called "professional," though other praise might be given to the occupa-- tion. Second, the occupation had to have a theoretical grasp of the phenomena with which it dealt. It was, in Flexner's view, an intel-- lectual enterprise. If it did have to rely upon clever hand techniques, it sought a generalized understanding of why they worked. Third, the occupation had to apply its theoretical and complex knowledge to the practical solution of human and social problems. Fourth, it had to strive to add to and improve its stock of knowledge. Thus, Flexner made research a major requirement, removing any consider-- ation of tradition–centered trades, the orthodox priesthoods, the partisan cliques and unyielding sects. Fifth, an occupation had to pass on everything it knew to new generations. This must be done deliberately and formally. Sixth, Flexner believed that a profession must exhibit the guild proclivity of organizing itself so as to establish discriminating standards and to regulate the behavior of its members. The seventh and final requirement for a profession is Flexner's mind was that it had to be imbued with an altruistic spirit. This may be interpreted to mean that any occupation governed by a quest for profit rather than the desire to serve could not qualify. And quite naturally when social workers, along with many others, were measured by these criteria, they did not qualify.

An additional Flexner requirement was that "the paramount function of a profession is to ease the problems caused by the relentless growth of knowledge." Who can deny that this is a prime function of librarians? Over the past several years librarians have begun to develop a body of knowledge, which though resting on the research and writings of other professions, is uniquely applied to the problems faced by a separate group. This is now borne out by our own research into the nature of libraries and library services.

It can safely be assumed, I believe, that the several institutions represented here today, despite their varieties, have one major interest -- the development of capabilities in students to make the most of their lives. As they present themselves to our "towers" of learning which have been implanted on the American psyche as the road to successful living, we find myriads of motivations and objectives among them. Some have already seriously mapped out their goals to the extent that they are ready to assume the responsibilities of sharpening their grasp of the selected subject matter so that their goals can be reachable. On the other end of the spectrum are those who find academic demands frustrating. They are on campus for a variety of reasons, including opportunities to engage in sports, to fulfill the dreams of their parents, or out of a mistaken idea that college will make no more demands upon them than the often mediocre secondary schools from which they have come. Often they have emerged from these schools with very low reading and/or comprehension abilities, but worse yet, with little or no realization given to this shortcoming as a deterrent to whatever dreams or aspirations they may have had.

In recent years, librarians have learned that this profession may not have a monopoly on some mediocre skills, but that they have compiled a background of knowledge, which when matched with the specially developed skills of serving people become kind of special. It has long been my contention that as librarians gain standing among their academic colleagues with credentials that count, they then have an opportunity to write their names in the annals of educational history by the type of superior service they provide. It meant, however, that as a group we had to develop pride along with academic credentials. We had to be convinced that the service we were rendering was important to the teacher/learning process before we could properly sell the idea of our expertise to those responsible for administering the institutions.

Just as other occupations have developed a keen sense of pride in their work, there may be similar occurrences in the library profession. I know a documents librarian who not only knows a great deal about materials, but has also developed a keen sense of supplying the needs of patrons. She is not only aware of what is in the documents, but is able to prescribe certain items somewhat like a doctor pre-scribes medicines. She takes pride in being able to open the eyes of students to what information is stored and is desirous of providing the key to getting at the miniscule needs of the moment.

Yesterday, representatives of a dozen colleges and universities with LSEP grants held a pre-conference here on the sole purpose of exchanging information. They were the fortunate recipients of Library Service Enhancement Grants from the Council on Library Resources. Throughout this year they have been assessing the needs of their campuses for library services. They have talked with faculty, students, and administrators in order to get a "feel" for the needs as they exist among their patrons. That survey was followed by a period of planning, a period in which librarians were able to come to grips with problems facing the academic structure, and to which they could bring their expertise to bear. They have faced up to such problems as the reluctance of students to use available resources. They have had to deal with problems of students who are unable to read sufficiently well to cope with academic expectations. But more importantly, they have applied their own research and knowledge to the problem, gathered input from other faculty and administrators concerned, and have in many instances been the catalysts for viable programs to serve this group of students. They have had to come to grips with the power of ideas as an aid to overcoming the lethargy brought to campus by some students. Convinced that providing the right kind of reading materials and inciting a spirit of inquisitiveness in students can often lead to accelerated learning, these librarians are now on the front line of attack against direct problems of academics.

I contend that our claim to professionalism rests primarily with our abilities to apply new and innovated thinking to the whole spectrum of education. One way of approaching this in a broad way is getting involved in the whole teaching/learning process. If the problem is discerned to be a too low expectation of students, we can try to bring attention to it, while providing students with challenging new materials. If there is a problem with the commuting student, then we can focus upon the library's role in finding solutions. Any cursory examination of recent library literature will demonstrate librarians' concerns with the totality of educational problems, from budgetary suggestions to financial assistance.

Recent years have witnessed a large scale concern of librarians for data processing. Other applications of industrial and commercial techniques to assist in the delivery systems of libraries are now commonplace. Librarians are in a good position to understand that iso--lating these from the experience of students is to hinder their academic growth and development.

Librarians certainly played a large role in the development of the idea of federal aid. Look at the influence we had upon legislation leading to the Higher Education Act of 1965, and the Elementary and Secondary School Act. Our organizational lobbyists gained the attention and plaudits of other lobbyists by the way they pursued their unselfish objectives. Now, a few years later, young people living in isolated areas are at least exposed to books where a few years ago they were noted for their scarcity. They are employed in thousands of positions which were literally created out of the federal monies being shared with schools to improve basic education.

Despite these demonstrations of professionalism, many of our number are still relegated to positions akin to any other technical position. I hold that institutions which deny librarians an opportunity to contribute are choking themselves by failing to utilize available talent. Too many of us are still excluded from important considerations where policies are being made. We might ask how one expects an institution to have a strong academic program when the librarians are frustrated by not being provided opportunities to fully participate in the structuring of educational policy.

In each of my appearances before these annual conferences I have urged librarians to get involved with the teacher/learning process. It is heartening to note that progress is being made. My voice is only one among many supporting this concept. Where they have been heard, educational programs have been strengthened. Where they have not, such programs are likely to be faltering. Complacency on one level or another causes libraries to continue occupying second and third priorities in consideration of library support.

During the last century Thomas Carlyle wrote that "the place where we get knowledge, is books themselves! It depends on what we read, after all manner of Professors have done their best for us. The true University . . . is a collection of Books." In my time, B. Lamar Johnson became a leading exponent of books as the core of the educational program while at Stephens College in Missouri. Louis Shores introduced the idea of The Library College in 1933 when he spoke at an ALA convention. Harvie Branscomb wrote that "there has been lacking a sense of common purpose and, consequently, attention to the problem of the most effective coordination of effort."

Our interest is much more than instruction in the use of libraries. Our real concern is the full development of minds to their maximum potential. We recognize that to neglect the inculcation of proper respect for and understanding of ideas, future generations of our people will be handicapped. As is pointed out in a popular tele-vision commercial, "a mind is a terrible thing to waste."

I do have some specific suggestions to make for becoming more fully involved in the educational process, or for filling the void which too often exists when educational programs are planned without the inclusion of the librarian's point of view.

First, I would cajole you to keep abreast of issues which face colleges and universities. This can be achieved by reading a selection of periodicals which concern themselves with the problems of col-lege and university education, or education in general on a regular basis. Examples are: *The Chronicle of Higher Education* which each week carries significant news about higher education. Consider such recent articles as "Two Year Colleges Prepare to Fight for New Clientele;" "Colleges Toughen Requirements That Students Show Basic Skills;" "Broader Support Possible for Scholarly Publishing." These are not articles about libraries, but they will each indirectly effect the library programs. Changing attitudes about higher educa-tion are reflected in the monthly issues of *Change Magazine.* The May 1977 issue carries some interesting reading on open admissions at New York's City College, along with articles attempting to clarify resistance to federal controls at Wheaton College and at Brigham Young University. International education is enriched by informa-tion on changes in the higher education program in China. The *AAUP Bulletin* for February 1977 carries an article which begins by asking the question, "Where Is the Small Private College Going?" It begins with the statement, "I have been puzzled in the past few years about the lack of decisive direction in many private colleges. Administrators, faculty, and students in small private colleges are becoming less and less certain about how and why they differ from their counterparts in public education . . . The cry is heard that for small private colleges to survive they must justify their existence by showing themselves to be in some important way unique." Each of these issues has their importance, and each is more relevant to some than to others. Do librarians have any interest and concern in such problems?

Second, develop at least a general knowledge in a specific field which appeals to you. If your interest happens to be in political science, I suggest regular perusal of such magazines as *The Center Magazine,* published by the Center for the Study of Democratic Institutions. A recent issue carried an article on "The Life of Literature" in which an assistant professor of English at the Univer-sity of Pittsburgh raises some pertinent questions about why litera-ture is important to all of us. The same issue carries an article by Mortimer Adler entitled "Which Are the Classics?" asking the ques-tion, "Which authors of our century will endure?" and "Whose works deserve the designation 'classics?' " Not only should this be read by librarians but it should be called to the attention of those responsible for curricula in our colleges.   Other suggested specific areas which deserve our attention are: a) Students entering college who cannot read well enough to keep up; b) the expansion of curricular offerings in light of developing interests and needs of society; c) programs for the gifted and the physically handicapped on campuses; d) the teaching of humanities on campus -- how much or to whom?; e) programs in the liberal arts; f) education for jobs. These are just a few suggestions. I am sure that you can think of many more.

Third, develop your own sense of professionalism by applying your background in library science to any problem facing the institution. Then try to follow through by getting involved in finding solutions. I still like the idea of cataloging the interests of faculty members and then calling their attention to articles and books which they might be able to utilize in the enrichment of their teaching or research. We see so many more (or should) materials than they, and in this interdisciplinary age, an article of interest to a natural scientist might appear in a periodical published primarily for social scientists. Certainly what we do for a faculty member will be reflected in his teaching, therefore reaching many people.

Fourth, demand some time away from the desk, time which can be used pursuing professional interests. How much waste still exists in libraries where well--trained librarians are forced to spend so much time in unrewarding pursuits? Make sure that library programs encourage professionalism. I find that many library directors actually discourage the intellectual development of members of their staffs by placing all kinds of discouragements in their way. Try to avoid the boredom of underutilization of your talents. If you are really concerned, you will find a way to do something about it.

Fifth, be yourself. Once you have determined your ambitions, your concerns, weigh them against the possibilities. It matters not what others think about you and your concerns, as long as you are satisfied.

If when you have gone from this place, gone from another annual meeting of orientation people, you have had your minds stimulated to do something about a particular problem in your library, and the better if a solution to that problem in your mind will bring about a strengthening of library service to those who need it, then your journey will have not been in vain. Change really is taking place, though some times it may not seem so. Look back ten years ago to what we had in comparison to the present and you will understand. And now I say, God bless you in your search for alternatives, for ways to infiltrate the educational establishment, and to un--

lock the doors of knowledge to all who knock. Remember Carlyle — "The true University . . . is a collections of Books." Librarians have the keys. Our job is to unlock, open wide, and encourage students to follow the dictum of Alexander Pope: "Drink deep, or taste not."

PROJECT LOEX
AND THE NATIONAL SCENE

Carolyn Kirkendall, Director
Project LOEX (Library Orientation/Instruction Exchange)
Center of Educational Resources
Eastern Michigan University

Now it's time for the annual report from your national clearinghouse for academic library instruction, Project LOEX.

First of all, I would be interested in seeing how many libraries in the audience participate in this exchange. Would you please raise your hands if your library receives LOEX *News* and/or you have contacted us for information or materials?

For the benefit of those present who are not clearinghouse members, the idea of a national clearinghouse for academic library instruction was conceived at the first of these annual conferences in 1971. By 1972 the exchange was a working reality and since January of 1975 we've been funded by the CLR. We collect, organize and dispense library orientation and instruction data and loan samples on an international scale, make referrals to library programs, provide exhibits for workshops, publish the quarterly LOEX *News* and assist instruction librarians in their research endeavors.

In your registration packet you will find a LOEX data sheet. On the reverse of this sheet is a selected summary of member activities which I thought you might be interested in reading. Percentages on this latter sheet are generalized. Statistics on the data list, since it was printed a few weeks ago, have, naturally, altered. Current statistics as of yesterday: 642 members, 8842 sample materials, and so far this year we have circulated 6269 items.

Any credit which our office could claim from this expansion in size of collections, contacts and services is due directly to your participation. At this time I would like to express an official thank you to all of you who have deposited your library's instructional materials and who continue to participate so loyally and enthusiastically in this exchange.

Since last year, and in part again like last year, certain trends in library instruction activity have emerged. From our viewpoint as a central collection agency, LOEX can identify particular activity. First, interest and participation in bibliographic instruction continues to expand. You've already heard how instruction on a national level is firmly established. For mulating objectives for any facet of a pro--gram remains an initial and essential step. Altering those objectives as the library collection, staff and audience (patrons) change, or maybe the librarian himself/herself continues to learn, is also more prevalent.

Existing programs happily continue to be refined. We can also identify some complex programs which are now being simplified. This emphasis on returning to the basics -- to the methods which really work -- is quite wide-spread and results from a welcome iden--tification of the real role of instruction -- to provide the academic library user with instruction at the point and time of need. It's been almost a year since LOEX received the kind of letter that says -- please give me only the names of those libraries which are doing something really unique. We would much rather identify libraries which are establishing or refining basic instruction activities success--fully.

More libraries are keeping accurate records -- statistics which will assist the development of their programs. The need for reliable, standardized evaluation techniques and forms still exists and will continue to be the current area most in need of our attention.

Many instruction workshops and sessions have been held since January. More research by post--graduates and practicing instruc--tion libraries in the U.S. and several foreign countries is being con--ducted presently.

Materials deposited with LOEX reflect growing interest in, specifically, the search strategy, in library skills credit courses, in tailored, assignment--related exercises, and, as usual, in the path--finder approach.

State, local, and regional clearinghouses continue to be esta--blished and developed, both in the U.S. and in England.

As the rate of growth of academic library instruction programs expands, so does the LOEX workload. There are some drawbacks to this kind of continuing momentum as far as our office services are concerned. We're running out of space to put the new materials, of newsletter space to list them, and out of time to complete all requests as quickly as we would like. When you consider the alter--natives, however, we're very pleased. The LOEX office this past year, in addition to the regular duties, have continued to compile and revise lists of instruction activity by discipline and method, we are collecting results of the current revision of the 1972 ACRL BI Status Report, and the samples and information we are receiving from this revision have assisted us immeasurably in keeping the LOEX data bank and our materials collection current and represen--tational. We continue to provide exhibits when requested, and I am more than willing to accompany a display when invited.

We appreciate your response to our specific requests for ma--
terials in each issue of LOEX *News.* When we ask for particular con--
tributions, it means we really need them. We could still use more
samples of signage, proposals, copies of correspondence of faculty
contact, names of any persons engaged in a library research project,
any AV samples themselves, and would very much appreciate du--
plicate copies of handouts and materials which you routinely de--
posit.

Since the CLR grant expires this coming New Year's Eve, we
could also use your money! While we are still investigating potential
funding possibilities, it is not unreasonable to assume that after five
years of free clearinghouse service, satisfied customers might be
willing to pay a little for its continuation. In last September's issue
of the *News,* we included a kind of voter appeal in which we asked
you to let us know if your library might be willing to pay in institu--
tional subscription fee. The response was much more positive than
I had anticipated, in fact, a number of checks were received and are
being held. We are also considering subscriptions on a sliding fee
scale, the sale of materials kits, research projects, bibliographies, a
directory, and consultation services, and will let all members know
of our plans -- and our future -- as we develop these plans.

To conclude, it was not an instruction librarian but Walt Whit--
man who stated:

> "Books are to be called for, and supplied, on the assumption
> that the process of reading is not a half--sleep but, in the highest
> sense, an exercise, a gymnast's struggle, that the reader is to do
> something for himself. Not the book needs so much to be the
> complete thing, but the reader of the book does."

We must all share this opinion or we would not be in attendance
at today's meeting. If the past cooperation and participation of so
many LOEX members is any indication of a guarantee for the future,
then I am relatively optimistic, and predict that at midnight on next
December 31st, I will be able to say *Happy New Year -- Project
LOEX lives!* thanks to the support of librarians dedicated to the
promotion of bibliographic instruction in academic libraries today.

PROJECT LOEX REPORT

	1974	1975	1976	As of May 1977
Materials in Collection	1261	3834	7749	8842
Members	240	442	596	642
Friends	---	---	119	468
Requests for Information	64	279	892	518
Requests to join LOEX	---	136	668	76
Exhibits Provided	---	16	15	15
Letters Written (Excludes Requests Filled)	---	251	1178	445
Circulation	342	3795	9223	6269
LOEX *News*	2	4	4	1

INSTRUCTION METHODS

Tours	98%
Credit Courses	20%
Non--Credit Sessions	23%
Term Paper Clinics	10%
Any Evaluation?	53%
Videotape	9%
Lecture Sessions	80%
Full--Time Orientation/Instruction Position	8%
Part--Time Positions	81%
Separate Instruction Departments	4%
Instruction Within Reference Department	41%

TYPES OF LIBRARIES

Two--Year	24%
Undergraduate	24%
Undergraduate/Graduate	46%
Graduate & Special	6%

ENROLLMENTS

Under 1,000	20%
1,000 -- 5,000	40%
5,000 -- 10,000	16%
10,000 -- 15,000	7%
15,000 -- 20,000	9%
20,000 +	8%

PANEL

AN INTRINSIC INSTRUCTION ACTIVITY:
COURSE RELATED PROGRAMS
FOR SUBJECT MAJORS

PREFACE
Carolyn A. Kirkendall, Conference Coordinator

No matter which library instruction technique or method may be a favored approach of each of us, most of us basically believe that skill in information seeking ought to be essential for competent academic survival, and that the upper class student, in particular, benefits from instruction to make more effective use of the basic reference sources in his or her subject field. How many students majoring in psychology are familiar with *Psychological Abstracts*? How many seniors who will graduate with a degree in education have used *The Encyclopedia of Education* or *Education Index* or the *ERIC* sources?

To address these questions this afternoon, I am pleased to introduce four advocates of course--related library instruction for subject majors.

INTRODUCTION
Evan Farber — Director, Earlham College Library

I'm just going to make a few introductory remarks and then turn over the discussion to the three panelists.

Library instruction for subject majors ought to be the easiest, the most productive, the most fun of all the kinds of library instruction. It ought to be able to achieve what I consider the ultimate in course--related instruction, in this case course--integrated instruction: where the objectives of the librarian who is teaching search strategy, teaching a variety of access points to information, teaching bibliographic structure of a particular discipline, and the objectives of the course instructor ought to be mutually reinforcing. That to me is the ideal that we reach for.

Even though it's much simpler to work toward that ideal in instruction for subject majors, you do run into problems. I'm not

37

going to talk about the very obvious problems of working with particular faculty members, but let me just mention these problems briefly. First of all: the instruction to subject majors who have had no previous instruction. If they've had no instruction, how do we teach them even the basics -- the basics about using the library? The more advanced the student, and the more he knows his subject, the more blasé he's apt to be about basic library instruction, so there is first that problem about teaching the majors who've had no previous library instruction.

Secondly, there is the instruction for subject majors who have had some basic instruction before. Thirdly, there is instruction for advanced subject majors, assuming some previous library instruction in the subject itself and also a fairly sophisticated knowledge of the content of the discipline. You get those three possible levels of instruction and previous experience. Now the real problem gets to the subject major course in which you have a combination of these. You have some students who have had no previous library instruction, some who have had a little basic instruction and some who have had a fairly sophisticated instruction. How does one then talk about the sophisticated tools and talk to all of these people at once? These are some of the problems that one faces in talking on subject-related courses.

COURSE-RELATED INSTRUCTION
FOR EDUCATION STUDENTS

Hannelore B. Rader
Coordinator, Education and Psychology Division
Center of Educational Resources
Eastern Michigan University

Providing subject majors and minors with bibliographic in--struction is a most important and often gratifying task. Such stu--dents constitute an ideal group for this type of instruction because they are more sophisticated, motivated and intellectually curious than beginning level students and, therefore, their interest in bib--liographic instruction tends to be greater. Subject majors are ser--iously involved in their subject areas and frequently have to complete research assignments which involve sophisticated library use. This situation provides a perfect climate for library--related instruction because it is based on student--perceived needs. All of these points will help to sell course--related bibliographic instruction to faculty and ultimately, this will bring about active librarian--faculty co--operation. As has been stated previously, often the faculty is re--luctant to let librarians use class time for bibliographic instruction but when student motivation and needs are involved, faculty will certainly cooperate.

Course--related library instruction for education students is particularly crucial and needed because these students will become teachers in elementary and secondary schools and will teach thou--sands of children. The attitude of these teachers toward libraries and their knowledge or lack of knowledge of library skills will in--still library habits (either good or bad) in many future adults. Many of us are aware of the lack of library skills in elementary and secon--dary school populations around the country and we hear com--plaints of school media specialists about the non--cooperation of teachers when it comes to teaching library skills in schools. All of us can certainly testify to the lack of library skills of students who are entering our colleges and universities. Perhaps we can remedy the situation somewhat if all of us who work with education schools and colleges of education concentrate on providing library skills to education students before they graduate, and if we try to instill in them a positive attitude toward libraries. If we can train our future teachers to incorporate library skills into their teaching and to find their own information, to do their own research, to be able to evaluate information, to assess research critically and to under-- stand the bibliographic system in education, we will begin to conquer students' bibliographic ignorance on all levels. Who knows, we may even be able to contribute to teaching students to become indepen-- dent thinkers and learners.

Furthermore, I feel that the most effective method for such instruction is course--related because it is based on student need, it is timely, it is immediately applied learning and it is required as part of the course work. All of these factors are motivating the students to learn, and, based on various learning theories, these factors also work toward a better retention rate for the students. Course--related library instruction necessarily involves close faculty-- librarian cooperation and this will help us to do what A.P. Marshall discussed at lunch: to become actively involved in the teaching-- learning process, to share our particular kind of expertise with students and faculty in such a way as to enhance the teaching-- learning process and to graduate students who are prepared to cope with their own future knowledge needs.

Of course, there will be problems to be worked out when you are involved in course--related library instruction to education students. As Evan Farber mentioned, there are various levels of library knowledge within student groups and it is often difficult to deal with that. In the many years that I have been involved in library instruction, I have yet to come across a class of students who have the same amount of library knowledge. All the education classes I have worked with, from sophomore through graduate level, have included students who had no library skills knowledge at all, some who had some basic knowledge, and some who had a very sophisticated library background. However, the latter were always in the minority. This variation in knowledge makes suc-- cessful instruction very difficult because some students will quickly become bored (those who possess a great deal of library know-- how) and some will soon become lost because they lack necessary basic information. I have tried to overcome this problem by using a few minutes at the beginning of the class to dispense some basic library orientation information and to point out available print and media sources if more information is needed. Then I provide a brief orientation to the education collection such as arrangement and services. The major part of the session, however, is devoted to the bibliographic search strategies in education and how to find par-- ticular types of information as needed. This instructional session always includes information on the ERIC system and curriculum materials in addition to basic education indexes, abstracts and re-- ference sources. Students are encouraged to seek individual library assistance if needed after the instructional session. I realize that this is not an ideal situation. It would be much better if we could pre–test our students before they obtain library instruction and then group them according to levels of library knowledge for the actual instruction. In other words, a needs assessment is necessary for particular classes, groups and even schools and colleges of educa-- tion, and all of us need to work on this problem together with appropriate faculty to develop a proper mechanism for this. Some attempts have been published (see bibliography) but much research remains to be done in this area.

To combat both student and faculty apathy toward biblio- graphic instruction, we must also try to become involved in pro- fessional associations other than our own, such as the various ed-- ucational associations. This will help us to promote our point of view during meetings and workshops with faculty and to become aware of their professional needs and interests. Also, we must try to publish articles on bibliographic instruction in professional jour-- nals other than library--related ones because both faculty and even- tually students will read such publications rather than library lit- erature.

Library Instruction for Education Students
A Bibliography

Blumberg, Ethel L. "Library Course for Teachers." *California School Libraries* (May, 1963), pp.22--3.

Breen, Mary F. *Library Instruction in Colleges for Teacher Educa-- tion in the United States.* PhD dissertation 1954, University of Buffalo, New York.
Deals with the problem of library instruction, and how it is related to the aims and objectives of a library in a college for teacher education. Gives history of library instruction. In-- cluded are discussions of library handbooks, librarian--faculty cooperation, the library tour, library diagnostic tests and various types of library instruction. A long bibliography is also included.

Bristow, Thelma. "A Reading Seminar." *Education Libraries Bulletin* (Summer, 1968), pp.1--9.

Brown, J. "Assignment in Learning Analysis of Results of a Ques-- tionnaire re Library Related Content Included in Teacher Training in Canada." *Moccasin Telegraph* 17 (1974), pp.50.

Chapman, Geoffrey. *Prospective Manitoba Teachers and the Library.* Ottawa, Canada: Canadian Library Association, 1975. Oc--casional Paper no.84.
This work discusses the lack of library use instruction from elementary through higher education. The author points out the importance of library use instruction to prospective teach--ers. Education students at the University of Manitoba were tested on their library skills knowledge and found sadly lacking in this area. It is advocated that teachers and professors should be more library--oriented in their teaching.

Fidler, Leah Josephine. *Freshman Orientation Programs in Small Teacher-Related Colleges.* Master's Thesis, Indiana University, 1960.
Although most librarians agree that freshman college students need library orientation, numerous references in current litera--ture show that librarians are still trying to develop more ade--quate programs.
For this thesis freshman library orientation programs in small teacher colleges were studied and surveyed from 1957--1960. Ninety-five per cent of these colleges give some type of library orientation usually as part of English composition in freshman year. The lecture method is used, card catalog, indexes, and library arrangement are explained. Use of AV materials is found to be helpful.

Justis, L. and J.S. Wright. "Who Knows What? What? An In--vestigation." *RQ* 12 (Winter 1972), pp.172--174.
This article is based on a small sampling of graduate students at Oregon College of Education to assess their library skills. It was found that these graduate students were really lacking in the library skills area.

Knight, Hattie. "Case for Library Science in Teacher Education." *Malayan Library Journal* (November, 1963), pp.69--71.

Lancaster, John H. *The Use of the Library by Student Teachers: Some Factors Related to the Use of the Library by Student Teachers in Thirty-One Colleges in the Area of the North Central Associaton.* New York: Columbia University, Teach--er's College, 1941. 138p.

Larson, Thelma E. "Public Onslaught: A Survey of User Orientation Methods." *RQ* (Spring, 1969), pp.182--188.
This reports the findings of a 1967 random survey of 94 educa--

tion libraries of the American Association of Colleges for Teacher Education in the area of student orientation and pub--licity method were surveyed and summarized.

Line, Maurice B. *The College Student and the Library.* Southamp--ton, Great Britain: University Institute of Education, 1965.

Lee, Chi Ho. *The Library Skills of Prospective Teachers at the University of Georgia.* PhD Dissertation 1971, University of Georgia.
This study was designed to determine the status of library skills of University of Georgia undergraduates who plan to teach. It also tries to describe the current practices of library instruction for prospective teachers in teacher colleges in the Southeast.

Mangion, Marion B. "Need for Expanded Library Education Pro--grams." *Maine Library Association Bulletin* 30 (May, 1969), pp.3--5.

Parker, Franklin. "Library Resources for Educational Leaders: A Class Discussion." *Library--College Journal* 3 (Summer, 1970), pp.31--36.
This discussion took place in a graduate seminar composed of education majors, and concerns the need for library skills on the part of education students.

Perkins, Ralph. *The Prospective Teacher's Knowledge and Library Fundamentals.* New York: Scarecrow, 1965.

"Prospective Teachers Found Ignorant of Library Use and Re--sources." *Library Journal* 90 (May 15, 1965), pp.2348--2349.
Talks about Ralph Perkins' test of 4,170 prospective teachers at the University of North Dakota. He found that few students could make intelligent use of the library.

Rogers, M.L. "Library Project with Teachers in Training." *Top of the News* 18 (December, 1961), pp.19--24.

COURSE-RELATED INSTRUCTION
FOR HISTORY MAJORS

Richard Werking
Head, Reference Department
University of Mississippi Library

Why is bibliographic instruction important for subject majors, especially for advanced subject majors? Among the reasons are the following. First, it is probably at this point in an undergraduate's education that she will develop most as an independent learner. Second, such instruction can do a great deal to show students the personal nature of the research process and help them see them-- selves as contributors to that process. Finally, instruction to sub-- ject majors is a good method of educating faculty about biblio-- graphic techniques they may find useful, both for themselves and for their other students.

What form might such instruction take? The suggestions and propositions that follow are not applicable to all academic disciplines, but they certainly seem appropriate for history and at least some other social sciences. They originate from my suspicion that much bibliographic instruction, *including my own,* has really been "library orientation," showing students how to access the scholarly literature by using the various mechanisms the library makes available to its public for controlling packages of print (mech-- anisms such as the card catalog, *Social Sciences Index, Essay and General Literature Index,* etc.). A problem is that many access mechanisms to the scholarly literature, as opposed to the scholarly journals themselves, are not generated by scholars or addressed to their perceived needs. (Two externally--produced mechanisms that are addressed to those needs are the citation indexes and *Current Contents,* which make more efficient the scholar's habitual search-- ing methods -- looking at footnotes and browsing in journals). The result is that faculty members do not use some library mechanisms as efficiently as they might, because they have not considered them very relevant to their work. Consequently, they usually do not think to acquaint their students with them.

Bibliographic instruction for advanced subject majors should take into account the methods by which scholars locate the litera-- ture in a given field. At lower levels, students are taught to locate information and literature by using encyclopedias (general and more specialized), the card catalog, *Readers' Guide*, and *Social Sciences Index*. But at upper levels students presumably have some background in the literature of a subject, and they could be instructed to find the most relevant literature about a given subject differently, in the same manner that their professors do: 1) locate a few key works, perhaps a specialized bibliography, and certainly a review article if at all possible; 2) find other works cited in footnotes and bibliographies, and put together a core bibliography; 3) use citation indexes to update the bibliography; 4) consult recent issues of the most relevant journals, using either the journals themselves or *Current Contents;* 5) consult *Forthcoming Books.*

Before very long, the student could identify, not all the items in the literature, but those items which the practitioners in the field believed to be the most relevant. Almost invariably, in the history journals at least, these are the citations strung together in a very long first or second footnote to give the reader a historiographical context for the argument that is about to be presented.

The chief contribution of bibliographic instruction, however, is not to help acquaint the researcher with the issues and participants in a scholarly debate. It can be even more helpful by introducing two other kinds of materials: data sources, and literature that for one reason or another lies outside the conversation of most practicing scholars in the field. Instruction in these two areas will help students and faculty do more than summarize or synthesize the current debate; it may carry their perspective past it.

Several years ago, Thelma Freides wrote a very useful book entitled *Literature and Bibliography of the Social Sciences,* which unfortunately has failed to receive much attention in the bibliographic instruction literature.[1] Freides contends, and I agree, that it is helpful to distinguish literature from data in a social science discipline. According to Freides: "As used here, 'literature' refers to writings intended to analyze and comment on social life; 'data' refers to the written records of society."[2] Such data (or, if you prefer, "primary" as opposed to "secondary" sources) originate outside scholarly channels, are not as well controlled as the scholarly literature, and exist in massive amounts. Consequently, scholars are not well acquainted with the access mechanisms that exist for data. As part of bibliographic instruction to advanced subject majors, we should make the same distinction that Freides makes and introduce them to data sources and their access tools.

Such sources include the great variety of government documents (statistics, statutes, hearings, etc.), archival and manuscript collections, memoirs, newspapers, magazines, pamphlets, and machine--readable data bases. The access devices would even include the subject portion of the card catalog for headings such as "US--Statistics" and "US--History--Sources." In most other access tools for data sources, subject headings must also be confronted.

The second important body of material can shed additional light on the current debate in the literature. We should acquaint students with the existence of literature about which they are unaware because it is not cited in what the discipline has defined as the most relevant literature. This material may be relevant to the current conversation among scholars, but is not perceived to be by the conversationalists and consequently is not accessible via their footnotes or bibliographies. Some subsets of this genre include:

1) Older literature, such as articles in the *American Historical Review* or *Mississippi Valley Historical Review* from the 1920s or 1930s, or even some of the state historical journals, and accessible through *Writings on American History.*

2) More radical perspectives, particularly on issues involving public policy. Examples of such literature and bibliographic tools include the *Bulletin of Concerned Asian Scholars, Alternative Press Index,* and *Alternatives in Print.*

If the searcher has time, two other categories should be consulted:

3) Dissertations, located through *Dissertation Abstracts* and other channels.

4) Recent literature that is largely ignored, such as that found in many state historical journals and located via *Historical Abstracts* or *America: History & Life.*

At this point in the presentation the instructor could take a few minutes to draw the students' attention explicitly to the structure of the literature, somewhat in the manner outlined by Elizabeth Frick in her fine article.[3]

5) Most important, however, is acquainting individuals with a fifth subcategory: literature from other disciplines that would provide valuable and different perspectives on one's work. My own research about the origins of two federal bureaucracies early in this century would have profited from a more systematic approach to the organizational literature through *Social Sciences and Humanities Index.* And it is only at this point in a presentation, ideally, that I would talk to advanced subject majors about such tools as *Bibliographic Index, Social Sciences Index, Humanities Index, Essay and General Literature Index, Subject Guide to Books in Print,* and the *International Encyclopedia of the Social Sciences,* because I would expect these students to use them in a different way than would freshmen or sophomores, who are trying for the

first time to break into the literature of a topic. The advanced students are already there, or should be; they and their professors ought to be using these general access mechanisms to locate relevant material from *other* fields, to break into *those* literatures. We could thus show faculty the value, to their freshmen and sophomores as well as to themselves, of using such tools to help gain initial access to the literature in an unfamiliar field. In the process, by showing faculty some efficient ways of tapping the literature in fields other than their own, we just might help broaden the scope of some academic writing which, in general, is frightfully narrow.

Bibliographic instruction for advanced subject majors provides us with an opportunity. It can help us move away from what has sometimes been an emphasis at all levels on undifferentiated orientation to library materials, and toward a more selective, structured approach that combines attention to library resources with attention to pedagogy and user behavior.

NOTES

1. Thelma Freides, *Literature and Bibliography of the Social Sciences* (Los Angeles, 1973).

2. *Ibid.*, p.2.

3. Elizabeth Frick, "Information Structure and Bibliographic Instruction," *Journal of Academic Librarianship* 1 (September, 1975), 12–14.

COURSE-RELATED INSTRUCTION
FOR SOCIOLOGY STUDENTS

Sharon Rodgers
Social Sciences Subject Specialist
Carlson Library, University of Toledo

I would like the world to have ideal conditions for bibliographic instruction. But I am really back at the very beginning, I think, when compared with those who have been speaking. While I would *like* subject matter instruction to be intrinsic to our instructional activities, I am not sure at this point that it *is* that basic. We can make a logical, even impressive, case for such activities, but, in many situations in which we find ourselves, the market for our bibliographic instruction simply does not exist. We, as librarians, provide only half of the necessary equation. The course--related library demands from the faculty may not exist. This lack of de-- mand is my concern. I want to discuss the lack of demand and then talk about some ways we can generate that demand from the faculty.

First of all, most of us may be aware of developments in higher education that have made assignments beyond the textbook dif- ficult to plan and manage. Certainly we are aware of increasingly large classes that teaching faculty have to cope with. This may be much more apparent at larger institutions. It is most evident at the undergraduate level where term papers are not assigned in the di- mensions that they were in past years. The factor of large classes combines with problems of plagarism and purchased term papers to create a wide--spread hiatus in the assignment of term papers, the traditional library project.

Additionally, trend after trend of innovative ideas has washed over and through academia. Many of the streamlined styles of learning, such as computer--assisted instruction, self--paced instruc- tion or some kinds of competency approaches, have little place for a library component. The trend toward various forms of ex-- periential education, or "doing a subject matter," has contributed little to emphasis on library projects. Finally, faculty may be ig-- norant of library possibilities or lack imagination in planning library experiences that are alternatives to term paper assignments. This lack of faculty interest in the library has resulted in keeping students away from academic libraries in droves on many of our campuses.

Let me give you some specific examples of the dearth of library emphasis in academia and in sociology specifically. Many of you have seen the "Reports on Teaching" published in *Change* magazine, beginning in March, 1976. These reports are notable for their lack of comment on library--related experiences or any excitement about what we are excited about: bibliographic instruction. These reports have talked about simulation; they've talked about all kinds of computer applications; they've talked about film; they've talked about using science fiction; they've talked about integrated living and learning. But they *have not* been excited about the possibilities that lie in the major resources on any campus -- the library.

Two more examples are from books which support classroom work in sociology. The first, *Field Projects for Sociology Students,*[1] describes applications of many research techniques that can be used to supplement classroom experiences for sociology students. At the end there is finally one experience labelled "The Library Project." The authors explain that:

"In our own experience, the research in which we engaged during our undergraduate days consisted primarily of library work. Although this is an *essential* part of any scientific investigation, particularly in the preliminary phases of locating background material and formulating hypotheses, we feel that a preoccupation with library research inordinately restricts the students' firsthand experiences of social investigation.[2] "

There is no further indication of the importance of library research. It seems to be just another way of saying that the library is the heart of the campus. It is the heart of our research too -- but we don't really believe it.

There are many kinds of instructor's guides or student's guides that accompany the textbooks used in all the institutions we represent. *Doing Sociology*[3] is designed to accompany *Sociology*[4]. "Doing sociology" involves possibly everything but the library. In the introduction, the author says the library will be used three times as a source of data.[5] In going through the guide, I counted at least seven times when the materials the author is recommending could be obtained best from a library, but the students or the instructors using the study guide would never know it from the information given to them. Let me give you one illustration. In the chapter on urban ecology, the students are encouraged to map the parts of cities which are associated with different activities.[6] The first instruction to the student is to obtain a detailed map with no suggestion about where one might be easily accessible to them. The student is instructed to map about eight different activities based on their own knowledge. At the end, this cryptic question appears: "What sources of information might be used to supplement your own experience and to verify your impressions? [7]" What a limited way to hint to students about the richness of census materials. I don't know how the students or faculty using the suggested pro-ject are going to get to the appropriate census tract information that they could use to complete the assignment.

Now, what can we do about generating demands for library use and instruction in the undergraduate social science curriculum? We have several strategies that can be pursued both on an individual level where many of us have appropriate contacts and on a level of professional group activity where liaisons with other professional groups can be established.

First, we must continue to work with individual faculty on our campuses. However, we may want to single out certain faculty for more attention. For instance, we need to pay special attention to those faculty who are writing textbooks by talking to them about the possibilities for including library information in the work that they are doing. For example, in textbooks (here again, I am using examples from sociology), there will often be sections that explain the "tools of the discipline" or make suggestions on data sources, but rarely mention the library. Perhaps the people who are writing the textbooks can be convinced (or educated) to provide much more explicit, useful information to the text-book users. Another group that deserves special attention is the junior faculty who have the contracts to do study guides to ac-company major textbooks. They are often desperate for ideas because it is very difficult to do anything unusual with a study guide that will distinguish it. They may be grateful for any sug-gestions you give them for appropriate library projects. These are two ways of reaching a wider audience and creating demands for bibliographic instruction.

Second, we need to contact publishers of textbooks. Pub-lishers demonstrated their influence on the issue of combating sexist information in textbooks. Many areas of our curriculum have been revolutionized because of changes in the material that publishers now make available to faculty. We can use this as an illustrative model to work with publishers about including more library--related information in textbooks and study guides.

Third, we can generate demands for library use by working through the professional associations in the various disciplines and their divisions on undergraduate education. The examples that follow are from the social and behavioral sciences, but the trend also exists in other disciplines. The American Psychological As-sociation, for instance, has a division on the teaching of psychology in which anyone may participate without being a member of the association. The division publishes a journal, *Teaching of Psychology*, which often contains information and notes about teaching ideas; it might be a good place to submit information about bibliographic instruction. The American Psychological Association has just formed a continuing committee on undergraduate education which first met in April, 1977. It is clear that this professional group is turning attention to analysis of what it is doing in the classroom and we can be ready to work with them on doing that analysis and making our own contribution.

A brief survey of other social science disciplines displays the same pattern. The American Sociological Association has a project on teaching undergraduate sociology. The group meets at national meetings and has been sponsoring meetings and workshops at regional meetings as well. The American Political Science Association has a Division of Educational Affairs that publishes a small newspaper called *DEA News* -- a publishing possibility for those of you who are building resumés. The Association of American Geographers continues its record of solid support for library programs by offering a series of papers on building library programs that you may be able to introduce to some faculty on your campuses. The American Anthropological Association cooperates with the Council on Anthropology and Education to publish the *Council on Anthropology and Education Quarterly*.

We need to reach beyond our own professional group, to create dialogue with other professional groups. We can publish in their journals. We can co--sponsor sessions at their professional meetings. Perhaps we could try to staff a booth in the exhibit area at their meetings. There are many possibilities for outreach that we need to explore.

I think we can have an influence on this wider audience to create opportunities for bibliographic instruction. We are in a position to see new data and new information sources. We can analyze these resources and suggest ways in which they can be used for teaching and research. Further, we are in a unique position to see what other faculty are doing. We can identify faculty who have good ideas for library projects and work with them on writing up those ideas for dissemination to a wider audience.

I wish you all a busy time and many publications.

NOTES

1. Jacqueline P. Wiseman and Marcia S. Aron, *Field Projects for Sociology Students*. Cambridge, MA: Schenkman, 1970.

2. *Ibid.*, p.v.

3. Dorothy Broom Darroch, *Doing Sociology.* New York: Harper & Row, 1973.

4. Leonard Broom and Philip Selznick, *Sociology: a Text with Adapted Readings, Fifth Edition.* New York: Harper & Row, 1973.

5. Darroch, p.5.

6. *Ibid.*, p.110.

7. *Ibid.*

TEACHING AND LEARNING METHODS FOR
BRITISH LIBRARIANS

Nancy Hammond
Library Education and Training Officer
Polytechnic of North London

The purpose of this paper is to discuss various British projects and courses concerned with teaching and learning methods.

More specifically, I would like to tell you about some short courses run by a number of institutions in Great Britain; the SCO-NUL tape/slide scheme; a British Library project entitled: "An Investigation of Librarians' Needs in Relation to Teaching and Learning Methods;" the Travelling Workshops Experiment; a bit about what is happening, or not happening in the Schools of Librarianship; and at the end a few Do–It–Yourself ideas.

SHORT COURSES

In the United Kingdom a number of short courses on subjects related to teaching methods are run either annually, occasionally or as the one off sort of thing. A comprehensive list of short courses in Great Britain is now being included as a supplement to *Library Association Record.*[1] The first of these is in the April 1977 issue. A more specific listing for our purposes is to be included in the new newsletter from the Information Officer for User Education who is supported by the British Library. In volume 1, no. 1 April 1977 issue of *Infuse,*[2] Ian Malley, the Information Officer writes, under the heading Conferences, Courses and Seminars Forthcoming, "This calendar will first of all include all conferences and seminars related to user education. It will also include courses of two sorts: firstly, there will be practical courses on library and information techniques aimed at practitioners e.g. "Using the chemical literature." Second-ly, there will be the courses which are concerned with teaching and learning methods for librarians e.g. "Closed circuit television and video tape." Notable in this first issue of *Infuse* are the courses run at the College of Librarianship Wales on Tape/Slide production and video tape. While reading in "Library Instruction: A Column of Opinion"[3] of the problems of creating a tape/slide at Parkside Library at the University of Wisconsin, I wished the authors had been able to attend such a course.

In connection with this type of short course, during my year as a Tutor Librarian at Hatfield Polytechnic, I attended an in--service course for new lecturers run by the Polytechnic. The course ran for one week before the Autumn term began, and then one day a week during term time for the remainder of the year. It was run by a member of the Humanities Department who had a Ph.D. in Educa--tional Technology. I will always be grateful to Dr. Ann Hawkins for making me aware that although during most of my schooling, teach--ing meant someone standing up and talking at me for an hour at a time, this was not necessary.

On Monday in the first week of the course we were told that on Thursday of that week we would each give a fifteen--minute talk to the rest of the group on any topic of our choosing. I was one of a group of ten, but the only librarian. Fortunately as we were all in the same boat, we were incredibly kind and helpful to one another. This, of course, is not a typical classroom situation, but for me, it was the best help I could have had at the moment. So before the term started I at least suspected that I could speak to a group of students or staff.

During the year we had opportunities to try out many types of teaching methods other than the lecture. In this context, Donald Bligh's *What's the Use of Lectures*[9] was an invaluable source of ideas. In addition, extensive coverage was given on the use of audio--visual aids, the advantages of team teaching, and the study of informal methods of presentation.

These in--service courses are given at many universities and polytechnics in the United Kingdom and hopefully they exist in the United States as well. I can see no reason why teaching librarians should not attend; and with a little tact, perhaps we can convince the teaching staff of this as well. In Britain both the University of Surrey[5] and the University of London[6] run week long courses be--fore the autumn term for lecturers from all over the country and from overseas as well, who want to improve their teaching perfor--mance. As a sidelight, this is a wonderful opportunity for a librarian in this situation to meet lecturers and to "indoctrinate" them about library education.

SCONUL TAPE/SLIDE SCHEME

The tape/slide scheme run by SCONUL, the Standing Confer--ence on National and University Libraries, was launched in 1970 and the following are the essential features involved in the production of materials. Each presentation is the responsibility of a small working party consisting of representatives of two or three libraries. One member normally undertakes the actual production work and must therefore have access to facilities for producing slides and making recordings. The other members contribute ideas, comment on draft scripts and assist in criticism and evaluation. Subjects which are suitable are ones which will be of interest to many libraries. These include case studies in the literature of specific subjects, guides to particular types of literature, such as abstracts or reports, and guides to the use of major reference works. Further details can be found in the SCONUL publication, *Tape/Slide Presentations: Recommended Procedures*, edited by Frank Earnshaw.[7] This booklet is being updated and expanded and is to be published again in the near future. Ann Aungle and I have contributed a very short piece in the new edition which we have entitled, "Tips for Tape Sliders, or Things We Wish We'd Always Remember."

There are now sixteen tape/slide guides which are available with a further fourteen in active preparation and twelve more in the planning stages. In the first round of productions librarians were only just beginning to get used to the method and did not always have access to good audio-visual facilities. However these early productions enabled a large number of librarians to see what others felt appropriate in a particular subject area.[8]

In discussions with librarians throughout the United Kingdom, I find that many make use of the tape/slide presentations which have been produced. Some use the slides to illustrate points in their own lecture. Others use them as prototypes for making their own tape/slides on the same or similar subjects. The scheme has been successful in helping librarians find out which sources and which points other librarians working in the same field are emphasizing in their work with students. It has provided tape/slide material for libraries which do not have the facilities to make their own, and it has provided a cooperative experience among librarians from universities and polytechnics who are interested in the same subject areas or the same problems of explaining sources to students.

Nancy Fjallbrant at Chalmers University in Sweden has recently published an article on "Teaching Methods for the Education of the Library User."[9] In this article she discusses the use of the SCONUL tape/slide productions in Sweden and the reactions of the users to the presentations. She reports on the evaluation tests done by the Swedish College of Librarianship and concludes that Swedish user reactions to the tape/slide medium were very positive.

Originally the tape/slides were seen as self teaching aids to be made available to students. However, the concensus of the SCONUL Tape/Slide Group's Exchange of Experience Seminar held in March 1976 was that the tape/slide material should be used in conjunction with seminars, discussion and practical work. An extremely interesting recent article which expands on this idea is written by Roy Adams of Trent Polytechnic Library and is entitled: "Teaching packages for Library User Education."[10] It was agreed, at the Ex--change of Experience Seminar, that there was a need to develop teaching packages including not only tape/slide but other materials and media. It also recognized that the human interaction between tutor and student might still be the most important ingredient of the "Package."

BRITISH LIBRARY PROJECT

The British Library is funding a project run by Dr. P.J. Hills of the Institute of Educational Technology at the University of Surrey. It is entitled "An Investigation of Librarians' Needs in Relation to Teaching and Learning Methods." The project is being carried out by a small working party on which I serve. We meet about twice a term and carry out actions decided upon whenever we can fit them into our own schedules.

The first task of the working party was to attend the University of Surrey's Course on Teaching and Learning in Higher Education held in September 1975. We were the first librarians to participate in this course. It is advertized as suitable for more or less experi--enced teachers, but not for totally inexperienced teachers, and in addition, for teachers in all subject areas and in all branches of ter--tiary education. Our aim was to evaluate the course in terms of its usefulness to librarians. We met regularly during the eight day course to discuss our reactions to the sessions and at the end of the course we each submitted a written report to this same end.

Some of the areas covered during this intensive course were: the lecture, small group teaching, discussion groups, educational aids, aims and assessment in teaching, how to study, self teaching, making a video tape, tape/slide preparation, and practice lectures. Many of the practical sessions were run for groups of about eight. For these sessions we each were members of separate groups. This provided us with an opportunity to react to, and get the reactions of, the largest number of teaching staff possible. I found this to be one of the most valuable side effects of the course. Most of the lecturers were amazed to find out that librarians were teaching, as well as the sort of things they taught. Yet another chance to "in--doctrinate" academic staff.

The concensus of the librarians that attended the course was that almost all of the sessions were pertinent to librarians, but that some further discussion among librarians would be useful as well. It was agreed that there was a need to develop special courses for librarians either on their own, or in association with members of academic staff. One design which was discussed might include a 50:50 ratio of librarians and members of academic staff. The pos--

sibility of running a pilot course has been discussed. It was decided that a questionnaire should be circulated to librarians in the UK who were involved in user–education to determine: 1. What teaching methods they were using; 2. What other methods they would like to learn to use; and 3. What courses on teaching methods they had attended or knew of.

The conclusions derived from the 174 questionnaires returned were that although a large number of respondents indicated they used tape/slide and practical exercises – these two, plus video tape, film and programmed learning were high on the list of items they would like to learn to use. The answers to the third part indicated that courses in the area of teaching methods had been fragmentary until now.

A report on the project will be published in mid–1977. It has however become apparent that:

1. Librarians feel a need to know about the large variety of teaching methods that now exist.

2. At present there is very little direct supervision of courses in the UK to take account of this.

Similar ideas have been recently stated in an article by Malcolm Stevenson, "Education of users of libraries and information services" in*The Journal of Documentation*.11 He says, "There is, however, a problem in that librarians are not skilled in educational techniques. Indeed many librarians have chosen not to teach. It is essential therefore that librarians involved in user education be themselves educated for the job. Apparently such education is not given at library school, though it may be the case that this training is best suited to a post–experience level course. It appears however that no such suitable course is available."

The project has recently made a proposal to the British Library to continue our funding through Spring 1977. We have some inter–esting plans for further devleopments in teaching and learning methods for librarians and hopefully our proposal will be approved and we can carry on with them.

TRAVELLING WORKSHOPS EXPERIMENT

A recommendation was made by the Committee on User Educa–tion of the British Library Research and Development Department to support an experiment to assess the effectiveness of travelling work–shops as a means of teaching information handling skills to under–graduates in universities and polytechnics. It was thought that one institution would set up and operate a workshop facility to visit a number of separate institutions. Courses were to be provided in biology, mechanical engineering and social welfare. The aims of the project would be to examine the feasibility of travelling workshops and their effect on host institutions; to demonstrate various ap--proaches and methods, encourage future developments in the area of reader instruction; and to make recommendations for future work.

A proposal to run the travelling workshops by Newcastle upon Tyne Polytechnic Library was accepted early in 1975. The project was to run from July 1975 to August 1978. It would be staffed by a project leader, three specialist teaching staff and clerical help.

Courses would be run in universities and polytechnics and sim--ilar institutions in Northern England and Southern Scotland (about 30 in all) during the second and third years of the project. The first year was to be devoted to preparation and testing. The Aslib Re--search and Development Department was commissioned to assess the effects of the workshops on participants and the effectiveness of travelling workshops in user education generally. At the same time the project team would be expected to evaluate teaching methods and materials used.[12]

One of the project objectives has been to demonstrate to teach--ing and library staff how various aspects of information handling can be taught and incorporated into the student curriculum. This in--cludes encouraging a continuing program in the institution and furthering library--departmental co--operation to this end.[12]

In January 1977, after nine workshops had been run, the Ex--periment issued the following statements regarding teaching methods and materials. 1. A formal lecture method of presentation, par--ticularly one in which emphasis seems to be placed upon a biblio--graphical tool, for its own sake, is not favoured. 2. The workshops, indeed bibliographical sources generally, are seen as purely instru--mental, the means to the end of successful projects, dissertations, etc. 3. For both of these reasons, students prefer doing practical work, rather than being passively instructed. This is particularly important in view of the novelty of many tools, or even types of tools, being discussed.[13]

By April 1977, fourteen workshops had been held in ten institu--tions of higher education. A further nine workshops are planned for this spring, and nine more will be held during the next academic year (1977–1978).[14]

On the 22nd of April I attended the second day of a two--day Biology workshop run by the project at the University of Stirling in Scotland. I was able to see how the workshop ran and something of the student and staff reactions to it. The students were mainly third year biology students along with a few postgraduates. The setting was a large meeting room near the library. The students were free to come and go as they wished. The first day of the session began with a few remarks by Daphne Clark, the biology subject specialist, who has developed the materials with the help of her colleagues. These now include a part–time graphic designer who has joined the team. The students were then shown a tape/slide presentation Using Biological Information. Each participant received a workbook of instructions and practical exercises with which he worked through all the materials on display. Various aids were used throughout to explain how to use the different tools. For example, searching Biological Abstracts was explained by a simple wall poster as well as an audio–tape guide to its use. Chemical Abstracts had a special tape/slide sequence on its use for biologists. The subject specialist was there throughout the workshop to answer questions. Pre– and post–tests were administered.

At the end of the second day there was an evaluation session. The students, library staff, and workshop members discussed the value of the session. The students were very enthusiastic. Many expressed a desire for this type of instruction earlier in their course. The fact that all the tools were set out together meant they could see the full scope of tools in relation to their course. Some of the library staff that attended pointed out that almost all the tools were readily available in the library, and if the students had asked, they would have been shown how to use them. The students answered this with, "How can you ask if you don't know what the question is?" Many of the things on display they never would have dreamed existed. The one suggestion was that if the workshop could take place where full sets of abstracting and indexing services were available, they could have searched further in respect of their own topics. It seemed to me that the workshop was not only an extremely useful exercise for the students but also made the library staff more aware of the problems faced by the students.

The workshop team has now decided to change direction slightly. While many libraries who have hosted Travelling Workshops would welcome them regularly, others feel that it would prove too costly and they would like to develop their own courses. However, many have expressed interest in the learning packages and other materials which have been developed by the project, and are confident that such materials could form the basis for user instruction programs in any academic library.

Therefore the project team is now trying to find out how much interest there would be in the purchase of their materials and what other subject areas should be covered if other packages are prepared. To this end they are running two forums during July 1977:

July 5   University College, London
              (Engineering Building, Room G6)

Gower Street
London, WC1E 6BT

July 12   Manchester Polytechnic
             (John Dalton Faculty of Engineering)
             Chester Street
             Manchester M1 5GD

The learning packages and other materials will be exhibited in simulated workshops. Participants will be able to work through the packages in the three subject areas or simply examine the materials to assess their usefulness. Anyone interested in attending either forum should contact the Travelling Workshops Experiment, The Library, Newcastle upon Tyne Polytechnic, Ellison Place, Newcastle upon Tyne, NE1 8ST.

BRITISH SCHOOLS OF LIBRARIANSHIP

The situation in British library schools seems to be much the same as that stated in the Library Instruction column in the November 1976 issue of the *Journal of Academic Librarianship*.[15]

All my information on this subject comes from a conversation with Edward Dudley, the head of the Polytechnic of North London, School of Librarianship. In relation to a library instruction course being included in the post–graduate diploma in librarianship, he said that it was (1) not desirable to spend time on specializations in a one year course, and (2) it was not feasible because of the time available. There are 22 teaching weeks with about 200 lecture hours to devote to the whole of librarianship. However, it should be pointed out that the study of librarianship in the United Kingdom is developing in a slightly different way than in the United States. It is still on its way to becoming an all–graduate profession. Even now it is possible to qualify as a librarian by taking the exams of the Library Association and becoming a chartered librarian or ALA. It is then possible to do a dissertation and become a Fellow of the Library Association or FLA. The FLA is seen as equivalent, to a first degree and the holder of a FLA can study for a Master's degree.

A librarian with a FLA or a postgraduate diploma then can study for a MA or MPhil in Librarianship. Whereas in the United States the tendency seems to be to take a Master's degree in a subject area other than librarianship, in the United Kingdom the Master's degree in Librarianship is seen as an opportunity to do further research into a special area of librarianship. It appears at this time there is more interest by Master's degree candidates in "problems of use" than on actual user education.

DO–IT–YOURSELF

As this seems to be the state of affairs at the moment, it seems to me to be time to start from where we are and at least try to take one step forward. What can we do for ourselves? In my present position as Library Education and Staff Training Officer I work with our subject specialists on their user education programs. This can take many forms, i.e. team teaching, help with production of teaching materials, etc.

In addition, the staff training part of the job allows me to run three training sessions during each year. These often include reader instruction topics. On several occasions we have shown a video tape produced at the University of Leeds entitled "How Not to Lecture."16 In a very humorous way, frequent mistakes made by lecturers are pointed out.

One training session which turned out to be quite constructive involved all those who were interested in the teaching program. We met together as a discussion group. Experience of one member of staff can help someone else to avoid making the same mistakes. Several times I have helped Ann Aungle, our Media Resources Librarian, run sessions on how to use the media. The object of the sessions was to get all members of our staff to use the various machines without fear and trembling. It was during one of these sessions that we decided to show the introductory tape/slide guides to each of our six libraries. As we wanted everyone to have a chance to use the various machines we ran the session five times. About the third time we had seen the tape/slide guides we were nearly ready to scream. It was then that we conceived the idea of doing a Master Guide to the Libraries – mainly as a training aid for all those who would be involved in revising the guide the following year. We felt that the mass of detail given to the student in the introductory guides was a mistake. After all, everything important was written down in our Library Guide handout. We decided that our objectives in an introductory guide would be simply that the students would decide (1) that the librarians were human beings, (2) that they were approachable, and (3) that maybe the library would be worth a visit.

The guide was set to music to avoid all the problems of a script. It incorporated captions for the main points about libraries in general and about our library in particular. It includes as many relevant cartoons as we could find, plus pictures of our staff at parties and during their leisure hours as well as at their desks.

In the last two years the Master Guide has not only been shown to our own staff but at many courses, conferences and meetings throughout the UK. The time it took to produce seems to have been well spent, considering the enthusiastic response to it of many librarians. Compiling this program was not difficult or time consuming. We drew on existing collections of slides at our school of Librarianship, from slides we had taken at library parties, and some which we managed to convince members of our staff that they should bring from their own collections. "Do–it–yourself" is not only worthwhile but often fun as well.

In conclusion, I think that most librarians working in the area of reader instruction feel the need for instruction in teaching and learning methods. If it is not yet part of the library school curriculum and courses are not available or are too costly in time as well as money, we must all be on the look–out for programs, projects and experiments that will inspire us and our colleagues to make our own teaching programs more interesting and more effective.

References

1. *Library Association Record* 79(4), April 1977, supplement.

2. *Infuse* 1(1), April 1977, pp. 11–13. Obtainable from: Ian Malley, Information Officer for User Education, Library, Loughborough University of Technology, Loughborough LE11 3TU.

3. Soule, M.J. and Stoffle, C.J. "An opinion" in Kirkendall, C. ed. "Library Instruction: a column of opinion." *Journal of Academic Librarianship* 2(6), January 1977, p. 304.

4. Bligh, Donald A. *What's the Use of Lectures?* 3rd ed. Harmondsworth, Penguin, 1972.

5. For information contact: Miss D. Gray, Course Administrator, Institute of Educational Technology, University of Surrey, Guildford GU2 5XH.

6. For information contact: Gwen Heath, University Teaching Methods Unit, 55 Gordon Square, London WC1H 0MU.

7. Earnshaw, F. ed. *Tape/slide guides: recommended procedures.* SCONUL, 1973. Hills, P.J. ed. *Tape/slide presentations and teaching packages for library user education.* SCONUL, 1977. Available from: Secretary, SCONUL, Library, SOAS, Malet Street, London WC1E 7HP.

8. Hills, P.J. "Eight years of tape/slide guides for libraries." *Times Higher Education Supplement.* no. 279, February 2, 1977, p. 10.

9. Fjallbrant, Nancy, "Teaching methods for the education of the library user." LIBRI 1976, 26(4), pp. 258–9.

10. Adams, Roy J. "Teaching packages for library user education." *The Audio--Visual Librarian* 3(3), Winter 1976/77, p101–6.

11. Stevenson, Malcolm, "Education of users of libraries and information services." *Journal of Documentation* 33(1), March 1977, p. 63.

12. *News from: Travelling Workshops Experiment* no. 1, May 1976.

13.   *News from: Travelling Workshops Experiment* no. 2, January 1977.

14.   *News from: Travelling Workshops Experiment*   no. 3, April 1977.

15.   Kirkendall, C. ed. "Library Instruction: a Column of Opinion." *Journal of Academic Librarianship* 2(4), November 1976, pp. 240–1.

16.   Thody, P.M.W.   *How Not to Lecture.*   University of Leeds, 1970. Videotape, 30 minutes.

LIBRARY EDUCATION
FOR LIBRARY INSTRUCTION:
HOW THE PRACTITIONERS AND
THE EDUCATORS CAN COOPERATE

Charles A. Bunge, Director
Library School
University of Wisconsin—Madison

I am pleased to have this opportunity to share with you some of my thoughts regarding cooperation between library educators and practicing librarians. It should be obvious that the health and effectiveness of each of our operations depend on the health and effectiveness of the other and that cooperation can contribute to the well being of both. Today I want to talk very briefly about the structure of library school curricula, in order to provide a context for thinking about cooperation. Then I will mention some ways that practitioners can contribute their ideas and talents at the various levels or parts of the structure.

The curricula of the library schools with ALA—accredited master's programs differ in details, but are similar in broad outlines. At the master's level, the program usually includes a core of courses or learning experiences that is required of all students. In addition to this base or core, the program will include electives, and students may choose courses that allow preliminary specialization by type of library, functional area of practice, or a combination of both. As far as trends are concerned, we are currently seeing a great deal of study and experimentation with the required core, in terms of length, content, and instructional format. Also, there is an increasing interest in providing students practical experience as a part of the master's program. Finally, to accommodate expanding content, we are seeing a trend toward lengthening the master's program, sometimes by a summer term, but in a couple of cases schools are planning or operating two—year master's programs.

Many library schools, including my own, have advanced degree programs at the sixth—year specialist or doctoral levels. The content and structure of these programs vary widely, but they usually allow considerable tailoring to the needs of the advanced students and usually involve some research or quasi—research investigation. Finally, library schools have various types of non—degree continuing education programs. These can range from making regular elective courses available to practitioners for gap filling or updating (for example, a computer course or a government documents course) to institutes, workshops, and short courses.

How can practitioners share their ideas with library schools? There are a number of ways. First, many library schools have advisory bodies, on which practitioners serve. You might volunteer to serve on the advisory board of a school near you. Or, you could find out who the practicing librarians are on the advisory body of a school you wish to influence and contact them with your concerns and ideas. Schools like to hear from their alumni. If you have concerns about the curriculum or programs at your alma mater, call or write the head of the school or the subject specialist in your area of concern. For some things it might be most effective to work through professional associations. For example, the Committee on Education in Library Use of the Wisconsin Association of Academic Librarians developed a proposal for a course dealing with instruction in library use and urged the state's library schools to consider including it in their curricula. Some library associations have sections or divisions on library education where educators and practitioners can meet to discuss common concerns. You might join this unit and show up at its functions to share your ideas and concerns with educators. In short, communicate with educators at every opportunity. For the concerns of those at this conference I would suggest three targets -- the head of the library school, the reference teachers, and the teachers of the academic libraries course. They may give you a million reasons for not doing what you suggest (as you sometimes do when asked to extend service hours or to give that orientation lecture on Sunday), but if they hear enough to know that there is a need out there to be served, by and large, they will respond.

Now, how can you and library schools cooperate to get more people trained better in library instruction? Let's start with the students. One of our problems is the fact that not enough students have library instruction as a career goal to make elective course offerings for them a viable proposition. The students don't know the value of a course in library instruction until they are job hunting, and then it's too late. Also, students who do become interested in the field often lack the requisite background in communication skills and in educational concepts and techniques, so that what they need to be taught adds up to an impossible course.

You can help out in this situation by involving library student assistants or other students in planning and implementing your programs. Discuss librarianship as a career with them. Serve as role-models, making a career that involves library instruction an attractive thing to think about. And when you get someone who *is* thinking about librarianship as a career, point out that there are needs (i.e., jobs) in the library instruction area and encourage him or her to take courses that will provide background and skills that you wish you had or are glad you have, such as writing and speaking skills, educational concepts, etc.

With regard to the curriculum itself, it is my view that you should concern yourselves with the entire curriculum, not just an elective course in library instruction. For example, the required core. I believe that you should inform yourself and share your ideas on two fronts. First, what attitudes should all librarians, whether administrators, catalogers, or reference librarians, have, or with what concepts should they be familiar, in order for library instruction to become a fully integrated and effective part of library service? You want to make sure, don't you, that students see the teaching role of the library as one of its important functions? You hope that the re-- quired reference or public services course will include library in- struction as one of the key aspects of reference service, along with question answering and reading guidance. You can think of other attitudes and concepts that are important for all librarians to have, in order to create a total library milieu that encourages and enhances library instruction.

The other aspect of the required core that should concern you are the things that are taught there that are directly important to library instruction and that, if taught consistently and well, will not have to be taught (or can be taught at greater depth) in elective courses. For example, most or all core programs have elements that deal with the basic types of reference and information materials. You will want to work with library schools and particularly the teachers of this component of the core, to see that this instruction emphasizes bibliographic structure -- the kind of concepts that you try to get across in your pathfinders – and that it prepares students to teach about these basic sources as well as to use them to answer reference questions. Other examples could be cited also.

Moving on to the elective component of the curriculum, here too I believe that your efforts might take two approaches, i.e., taking fuller advantage of what is already in the course offerings and trying to get additional material made available. To make your in-- put here as effective as possible, I urge you to reflect on your own job, both your long--term hopes and goals and your day--to--day duties and responsibilities. What knowledge and skills are necessary and important for doing your job well?

In order to take advantage of what's already in library school curricula, share your conclusions, based on this reflection, with li- brary school students and their faculty advisers, in order that stu-- dents who are interested in library instruction will choose among existing courses as wisely as possible. Let's think of some things you might advise. Many library schools have a research methods course.

Would it be valuable for persons interested in library instruction to have such a course, where they might learn how research is done in various disciplines, how the library can contribute to research, and how to instruct library users to use the library and library materials in the research process? How about an audiovisual services course? Many such courses that library schools offer include laboratory components that familiarize students with a-v. hardware and teach some basic production techniques. What priority would you place on this? Some library schools have planning and evaluation courses. My reading of the literature of library instruction indicates that setting educational objectives, planning ways to achieve them, and evaluating the results are keys to the success of instruction programs. Mightn't important concepts and skills of this sort be learned in a general library planning and evaluation course? Other examples might be cited, but this will give you an idea of my thinking.

Turning now to the attempt to get library schools to add courses or learning experiences of relevance to library instruction, here too you can help in various ways. You will recall that I mentioned earlier that students and library educators are increasingly interested in the master's students' gaining field experience while in school. Would you be willing to work with a student, to provide him or her experience in library instruction? Many of your libraries are near enough to library schools that students could commute to work with you. Some of your campuses will be in session while library schools are on semester or other breaks. These circumstances offer opportunities for you to help a student be better prepared to work in library instruction upon graduation. If you are willing to take a practicum student, volunteer to the reference teachers, academic libraries teachers, or other appropriate person at the library school.

If a library school were to institute a master's–level elective course in library instruction, what should it contain? This question should inspire you to think and talk with your colleagues about what the beginning professional in this field needs to know. Having formulated some ideas, share them with educators. Perhaps the objectives and content for the courses you suggest would have considerable overlap with the needs seen by other segments of the profession, meaning that we might be able to design courses that would have a wider market and would be more viable from an administrative point of view than ones designed for one group alone. For example, you may be aware of a renewed thrust in public libraries toward helping their adult clientele learn new skills, pass equivalency exams, and otherwise educate themselves. Some of the needs of the public librarians for basic educational concepts and skills must be very similar to some of the needs of future library instruction librarians. Perhaps we need a library school course something like "educational concepts for librarians." Would you be willing to participate in planning such a course?

Another way you can contribute to the efforts toward elective courses in library instruction is to do research and publish the results, to enhance the content of such courses. I'm sure that you will be the first to agree that the literature of this field, while improving markedly, is repetitive and descriptive and sometimes difficult to use as the basis for a course. You are in a good situation to remedy this. Data that could be organized and used to produce knowledge passes through your hands every day. You could increase your own and your colleagues' effectiveness and upgrade the content of library school courses by conducting studies on the various aspects of your program and sharing the results.

I don't want to say very much about the advanced studies programs, except to invite you to be students in them. If you wish to specialize in library instruction, most advanced programs will allow you to tailor a program of courses and independent study, both within the library school and in other departments, to gain the knowledge you seek. Also, in relation to the advanced programs, I urge you to be cooperative with research efforts by advanced library school students. Answer those questionnaires, even if they do take precious time, and be hospitable if a Ph.D. student wishes to use your library as the locale for a study of library instruction.

In the area of continuing education, I think you will find library schools more and more interested in being of service; but here again we need your help. One of our most difficult tasks is what might be called market analysis, that is, identifying the specific needs to be met. Just what is it that you practicing librarians need to know or learn? How many of you are there with similar needs? As you work with your colleagues, in professional associations, conferences like this, or whatever groupings, discuss these matters and then share the results with the library schools. Perhaps the library schools and your colleague groups can work together to develop survey instruments to ascertain continuing education needs and reactions to various potential ways for dealing with them.

And finally, I believe that we need to develop a stronger commitment to continuing education among practicing librarians and especially library administrators. Our continuing education efforts can be successful only if we have students. All the good market analysis and planning in the world can be for naught if librarians cannot get time off to attend, if financial rewards and support are not available, or if librarians are unwilling to make personal sacrifices for increased professional effectiveness or for advancement. This is particularly true in the present economic milieu, where (as you all are only too aware) enrollments, credit hours, and the fees they pro duce are the name of the game for library education programs.

Well, these are some rather random thoughts on some ways that you might increase the effectiveness of library school training for library instruction. I hope they set you to thinking and encourage you to act. I know that many of you are thinking, "He still hasn't answered my question – why won't library schools listen to us?" Well, I think that they will. Just keep trying at every opportunity. Think your case through. Make both general and specific suggestions. Offer to help plan and implement. And, while you may not think you are getting through – just like you sometimes feel with your kids (if you have kids) or with your spouse (if you're married) – you will find that change will occur, and you will be happy to have had a part in it.

THINGS WE WEREN'T TAUGHT
IN LIBRARY SCHOOL:
SOME THOUGHTS TO TAKE HOME

Anne Beaubian, Mary George and Sharon Hogan
Reference Librarians and Bibliographic Instructors
Graduate Library, The University of Michigan

We are up here today as double agents, as full--time BI practi--tioners and reference librarians and as part–time library science faculty attempting to teach students the whats, whys, and hows of bibliographic instruction. For us the two roles are not just com--plementary, they are inseparable. We could not adequately teach BI to library students if we were not also teaching library use to graduate students. Furthermore, we believe that day--to--day in--volvement with reference work is central to both these teaching "angles." Our special vantage point makes us especially pleased with the dual theme of this year's Conference which considers both ends of the BI spectrum, that of library educators who can best provide initial and continuing exposure to instruction theories and methods, and that of library administrators who can best provide practicing librarians with the climate and experience they need to create successful BI programs. We feel strongly that a critical ex--amination of these two main sources of BI expertise is long overdue.

Take for example virtually all of us in this room. Who among us cannot boast -- or complain, if you will -- of the many "extra credits" we have earned, post–M.L.S., in the Graduate School of Hard Knocks, all in pursuit of excellence in BI, a term not in ex--istence when most of us attended library school? As pioneers we have all come to BI with conviction, enthusiasm, creativity, and not a little nerve – but without benefit of either theory or practice as part of our formal professional preparation. Of course, one can argue that pioneers by definition are those who set forth alone with scarcely any training for the adventures ahead. But the current wave of involvement in bibliographic instruction has been here for ten years now and shows no signs of abating, to the point where BI is mentioned in almost every public service vacancy announcement these days. Since people seldom advertise for pio--neers, it would seem that BI has come of age in the labor market at least. So do not we, as pioneers, with the assistance of the educa--tors and managers in the profession, have an obligation to share our hard--won insights and expertise with new generations of library science students so that they can enter the field with a basic under--standing of the rationale and methods of BI? We think so.

But let us first examine our premises more closely. Is instruc--tion being taught in the library schools? And the corollary ques--tion: Are library educators sufficiently aware of and sensitive to professional needs to give BI a permanent place in the curriculum? When queried on the subject, library educators are likely to defend their curriculum by stating that mention of instruction is "inte--grated" into reference or other required public service courses. Witness the less--than--whole--hearted responses of four library school deans surveyed by Carolyn Kirkendall for the *Journal of Academic Librarianship.*[1] But is mentioning instruction really enough? Is BI such an incidental -- or so obvious -- that it requires no exploration beyond an introduction? Hardly. Nor are we alone in our reaction to judge from our conversations with colleagues across the country.

A second premise to examine: Are most instruction librarians practicing without any formal education in BI, and does formal training and/or experience make a difference? A survey conducted by Sue Galloway two years ago in California and published in *Book-legger*[2] indicated that most librarians actively involved in instruction at that time had not received any relevant training for that role in library school. It is significant that Galloway's study included both older and more recent library school graduates, most of them working in an academic setting. Not surprisingly, Galloway's find--ings show that more librarians with prior classroom experience of some sort were teaching library instruction courses, and had done so for a longer period of time, than were those without such back--ground. So it would seem that experience does have a direct im--pact on a librarian's involvement in BI. Then too, recall the com--ments yesterday that library administrators who do commit them--selves to instructional programs often have trouble finding library school graduates who have had BI training and experience. All of which hints at the shape of some of the holes in both the tradi--tional library science curriculum and the traditional public service operation.

Don't misunderstand us. We did not agree to come here in order to bit the hands that feed us -- either of library educators or of library administrators -- but rather to suggest elements essential to the development of dynamic instruction librarians and ways to blend those elements into existing practices both in the classroom and on the job. True, in first contemplating the title of our talk we did come up with a long list of things we were not taught in library school but which we had to deduce, sometimes painfully, from experience. In fact, we had such a long list we forced our--selves to stop brainstorming. Then, in a positive vein, we decided to set down a complementary list of things that library adminis--trators and library schools can do to remedy the situation and con--tribute to the cause of better, more wide--spread bibliographic in--struction. We would like to outline both sets of reflections for you, welcoming your additions, corrections, and objections.

Four broad areas of librarianship, all vital to BI, seem to us to be insufficiently developed in the library school curriculum: the theoretical aspects of reference work, the role of the librarian as educator, the extended meaning of public service, and the intel--lectual responsibilities of the librarian as a professional.

Reference is part of the core curriculum in every library school and the basis of any BI program. Hence some of the difficulties encountered by BI instructors can be traced back to deficiencies in their formal reference training. Foremost among these deficiencies is ignorance of the dynamics of a search strategy, the construct by which one taps the flow of information in society. The literature of BI stresses the teaching of search strategy as an essential element in any but the most rudimentary instruction program, but this form of logic cannot be taught if it has not already been absorbed and practiced, as it must be whenever a student asks, "I need to write a paper on X; where do I start? " The appropriate response to which plea is for the reference librarian to suggest an efficient search strategy. Since this response involves a sense of probabilities and alternatives as well as "cold" knowledge of titles, it is an intellec--tual skill that should be conveyed throughout the library science curriculum. A great deal of the confusion expressed by librarians just beginning to do instruction stems from their own lack of focus about the nature of search strategy and its utility for the student.

Another commonly experienced deficiency in reference train--ing is in the area of reference question analysis. To resolve a com--plex reference question, one must be able to divide it into its parts, determine what type of reference tool can best answer each part, and locate specific relevant tools of each type. If a particular type of tool does not exist in a field, or does not include the informa--tion needed, the librarian must be able to devise alternative strate--gies. On a somewhat less sophisticated scale, BI seeks to teach students how to analyze their own research problems into basic components and recognize what types of tools are needed to handle the various components. To be an effective reference librarian, question analysis must be an automatic reflex. To teach that reflex to students, one must first understand the cognitive process.

Yet another curricular deficiency with regard to reference

concerns the concept of types of tools. How many of us were taught reference with a sheet of paper which had "Handbooks" on the top followed by a long list of titles without an explanation of what a handbook does? Or, to turn the situation around, how many of us were told what a handbook is but not what kinds of questions it can answer? A search strategy is constructed by building a pathway of types of tools, one leading to another. If reference librarians -- and BI students -- are to devise and manipulate search strategies, they must have a solid grasp of the characteristics of each possible type.

Related to a sense of types of tools is the understanding -- or lack thereof -- of how information is generated and communicated by society. It is crucial for anyone preparing to do reference work in an academic, public, or special library to comprehend not only information flow in general but information generation by discipline, the differences which exist between disciplines, and the bibliographic structure that parallels each discipline. With a thorough understanding of the intellectual history and dynamics of various disciplines, a reference librarian can more easily pinpoint probable sources of information. For librarian--instructors and their students, knowledge of the bibliographic structure of a discipline provides the logical framework for the development of a search strategy.

Nor do many reference courses sufficiently emphasize the communication skills which are necessary either to conduct a basic reference interview or to deliver an effective classroom presentation. It can be argued that interpersonal communication skills are more appropriate for psychologists or social workers, not librarians. However, if the librarian is to elicit specific information needs from the user and then explain in a non--threatening manner how to go about satisfying them, positive human interaction must occur. In a classroom, communication needs are multiplied many times over with the additional demand on the librarian--instructor to make an effective presentation of complex theoretical material to a diverse audience.

By and large reference faculty do not stress enough the revolution in technology which is already having a major impact on reference services. On--line union catalogs, computerized serials records, and the existence of bibliographic data bases must be understood and promoted by the reference librarian as a first--choice or alternative means of conducting research. Similarly, students in BI classes must be introduced to the coming changes in library bibliographic records so that they can use either printed or computerized formats with equal facility. If the librarian is uncomfortable or suspicious of mechanized processes, the student will pick up that anxiety.

In each of these cases, the new emphases we advocate in the reference curriculum are not suggested solely with an eye toward more effective BI, but from a broader educational interest which happens to have special importance for instruction librarians. We re-- cognize that ultimately the best and only sure route to expertise is via years of working at a reference desk and that library school cannot be expected to provide that depth of experience. However, it seems to us that at least some discussion of these dimensions can and should occur in the library school classroom so that when students begin a job they begin building on these ideas, not acquiring them in the first place.

While reference is a basic curricular offering in all library schools, and the specific deficiencies cited above should be cor-- rected in the interest of better reference librarians as well as better instruction librarians, our second target pertains especially to those present and future librarians working in an educational environ-- ment, be it an elementary school or a research library.

We are not convinced that library school students are instilled with the concept and ramifications of the librarian as educator. Education is an integral part of public service whether it involves explaining how to use *Psychological Abstracts* while answering a question at the reference desk, or teaching a classroom session on indexes as types of tools. For librarians, particularly those in an academic setting, to consciously regard and conduct themselves as teachers serves to reinforce the image of the library as a primary educational resource rather than as a dispensary of miscellaneous information. A study by Howell, Reeves, and van Willigen dealing in part with a correlation of user satisfaction with the reference librarian's mode of handling their questions suggests that "reference librarians can assist patrons more effectively when they consciously cultivate a teaching role as opposed to acting more passively . . . as information source." It is not so much that users' expectations of the role of librarians need to change, but that librarians need to sharpen their own self--perception and self--confidence in the teaching role.

To pursue the idea of the librarian as an educator further, we also feel the lack of user perspective. Many bibliographic in-- struction courses fail miserably because they are patterned after library school courses. We must always remember that library school courses are taught for future librarians; they are not intended for the layman. The whole sense of user perspective is somehow lost in library school, which is understandable since the goal is to train librarians, but once the librarian steps outside those Dewey-- covered walls, it is the user who is the prime concern. And the average user does not need or care to know the coverage dates of the *DNB* or when the *Readers' Guide* began. A whole shift of emphasis must occur if a BI program is to be successful, and a course or video--tape or practicum which would demonstrate to the library student the need for this shift would be extremely valuable in pro--viding a BI perspective.

Librarians who become bibliographic instructors would also benefit from an introduction to learning theory, testing techniques, curriculum planning, and media application. Most of us have never had education courses, and we could profit from an exposure to these topics which are essential to a well--designed BI program. Earlier in the Conference is was suggested that it is not appropriate for the library school to provide courses in the fields of education or psychology per se. However, all library schools are connected with institutions offering courses in those areas on such topics as writing objectives, testing, curriculum development, and the psy--chology of learning. It needs to be more strongly emphasized that courses such as these would be invaluable as cognates for anyone hoping to go into bibliographic instruction. Cross--listing of such courses is another way to bring their relevance to the attention of library students, a practice which seems to work at the University of Michigan and which we would strongly recommend.

One cannot make a good teacher, and we are not demanding that library schools produce "good teachers." We are only advocat--ing that a sense of the librarians as educator, user--centered attitudes, and means for developing teaching skills exist within the curriculum of all library schools. These approaches will help those students suited to a teaching role to prepare for library instruction jobs, while giving students who are not so inclined an understanding of the importance and complexity of the teaching function.

Although some would debate whether it is the place of the library school to prepare librarians to be teachers, there is a third sphere in which library schools do have an undeniable responsibility, a responsibility we feel is not being adequately met; namely, to de--fine the role of the public service librarian in all its many mani--festations and contexts. Most of us could describe the function of a cataloger in a library setting, but we lack the same sense in the area of public service. Library schools should do more to explore the various types and variations in libraries, not just descriptively, but as organic institutions each with distinctive demands on the public service librarian. Why and in what ways is a special library different from an academic library, and how do those differences relate to the communities which each serves? A broad, theoretical sense of the characteristics of public service in each of these settings would lead to improved public service planning with benefits for both librarians and the clientele they seek to serve. In a fractured, uncoordinated way, library schools do try to prepare students for working life as a community college librarian, or a medical librarian; library schools list many such specialized courses in their catalogs. But seldom is there a broad overview which considers the relation--ships of various types of libraries within a single community and the overlapping constituencies they serve. Is the role of the public service librarian viable in the real world? We heard yesterday that one of the impediments to the development of public service pro--grams may be the emphasis on technical service background in the selection of library directors during the last ten--to--fifteen years. If such hiring practices have indeed caused greater attention to be paid to the development of technical services, then perhaps it is time for library schools to provide a counter--balance by dealing in more detail with public service philosophy and responsibilities.

To focus the image of the public service librarian on the con--cerns of those of us here, we would like to have the library schools explore the role of the academic library within its distinctive edu--cational setting. Sangamon State is, of course, a stunning example of a library interacting with the totality of its institution. No doubt more libraries would like to adopt the Sangamon model, but most library school students entering the workforce have never con--sidered any alternatives to the traditional library organization they were exposed to in library courses. Once again, we refer back to the lack of emphasis on the librarian as educator, but now in the wider context of the library as an educational core of the entire campus.

The administrative planning and political considerations facing the public service director are very often glossed over in typical administration courses. There needs to be aggressive, long--range planning for both public and technical services, the kind of planning that can be appreciated if library students are challenged to con--sider the entire role of the library with its alternative goals and priorities and the many constraints affecting public service plan--ning (i.e., faculty pressure to maintain the book budget no matter what services might be sacrificed in the process).

The fourth and final area we would like to see strengthened in the library school curriculum concerns the role of the librarian as a professional. What is it to be a professional, and more specifi--cally, a professional librarian? Instilling a motivation toward con--tinuing education is certainly as important a task for a library school as actually providing courses, workshops, and seminars for librarians in the field. Library school students should be made aware of the many channels of continuing education that are available to them and should be encouraged to view continuing education not only as a personally rewarding experience, but as a chance to discuss and solve on--the--job problems with other working librarians. Library schools should also encourage an active involvement in professional organizations, perhaps by financing student attendance at ALA, SLA, ASIS, and other meetings. Students need to be formally introduced to the concerns and workings of professional groups, so that when they do take jobs they will be acquainted with the organizational structure and mechanisms for communication and problem--solving. Likewise, the importance of participation in discipline--oriented societies such as the American Historical Association cannot be stressed too much as an appropriate activity for the academic librarian, appropriate both for the individual's own satisfaction and for promoting the versatility of librarianship as an intellectual profession. Library schools can also encourage students to contribute to the literature, publishing not only in our, own professional journals but in those of other disciplines as well. A discussion of publishing patterns, the scope of various journals, and even manuscript preparation and style requirements are all basic topics. If the technical aspects of publishing were less mysterious, perhaps the task of writing would not be so overwhelming to the practicing librarian, and our journals would become forums for lively, meaningful exchanges. As one of the panelists said yesterday, it is particularly vital for librarians involved in bibliographic instruction to communicate ideas and techniques to one another.

Yes, we realize that all of us at this Conference have had different library school experiences. Some of you may have been taught all of these things; others may have been taught many of them. But most of us, we suspect, probably were not taught *any* of them, yet all are essential to effective instruction.

No doubt we could continue adding categories and items to this list until doomsday -- which may not be all that far off in higher education. However, we cannot really complain too loudly since obviously none of us would be here today unless we had all overcome these deficiencies on the job. But, as we all realize, overcoming them takes needless time and energy which can be better utilized in more forward--looking activities.

We would now like to suggest ways to remedy these deficiencies. Since there are two groups needing remedies -- the working librarian who, like all of us, has completed library school and who needs immediate help in filling the gaps of formal education, and the current library school student – it follows that there are two groups in a position to provide appropriate action, library administrators and library educators.

To begin with remedies which might be applied by library

administrators: these individuals must assume two burdens with re--spect to remedial education for bibliographic instruction. They must educate themselves so that they can knowledgeably initiate and manage a BI program, and they must provide BI--related education for their own staffs.

The responsibilities of an administrator in actively supporting an instruction program were covered well yesterday in the opening talk. To recap, an administrator needs to assess staff and resources to be able to make realistic short-- and long--range plans. An administrator must be willing and able to shift responsibilities and duties as necessary to free creative individuals to develop a BI program. An administrator needs to draw in resource people beyond the library's walls – audio--visual technicians, curriculum consultants, testing and evaluation authorities – who can provide expertise not available on the staff. An administrator is responsible for securing faculty and institutional support, political in the beginning if funds can be allocated out of existing library budgets, but ultimately financial if the program is to expand. An administrator must be willing to experiment with several pilot programs in BI so that the best combination of modes can be determined. An administrator will have to sensitize middle managers to the importance of instruction so that critical decisions affecting staffing patterns, clerical support, and acquisitions will be made accordingly. And, finally, an administrator can make future personnel decisions with an eye towards an active bibliographic instruction program as part of public services. Job descriptions should specify instruction duties and interviews should include questions pertaining to instruction so that candidates can be screened for their acquaintance with the basic principles of BI.

It is also within the province of the administrator to provide current staff members with the opportunity to become familiar with BI theory and techniques. One option is to send staff to in--structional conferences such as this one. What better way to en--courage enthusiastic – or even reluctant – librarians than by expos--ing them to an intensive session attended by "old timers" as well as novices? An administrator can also invite guest speakers and con--sultants to assess the library and institutional situation. There are activists all over the country who would be pleased to evaluate personnel, library resources, and the student population and to out--line a basic BI program. Staff can visit established BI programs in the area or contact LOEX or a regional clearinghouse for start--up information. Perhaps most importantly of all, an administrator can support – and perhaps demand – that staff involved in instruc--tion attend relevant continuing education courses and workshops. Apparently courses of this type are offered regularly in the United

Kingdom, as evidenced by the account of our speaker this morning, and one can only hope they will become more prevalent here in the near future.

In contrast to the library administrator's options, the possible remedies from the library education sector are somewhat more flexible since the business of education is inherently more fluid and its resources more easily shifted than those of a continuity-conscious and routine–bound library operation. We would like to see all library schools establish continuing education programs in the area of library instruction. We would also like to make some suggestions as to how library schools might better incorporate BI into their present overall program, and more specifically into their curriculum decisions.

Continuing education is a task that might properly be under-taken by a number of organizations -- CLENE, state library associa-tions, the recently formed ACRL Bibliographic Instruction Sec-tion, or regional clearinghouses, to name a few -- but foremost among the contenders would seem to be library schools for the obvious reason that they already possess the staff, resources, and expertise to provide such a service. It would be most natural for library schools to include BI workshops, seminars, and other such opportunities among their continuing education offerings. Nor is it unreasonable to extend regular or CEU credits to participants in such activities. Several large professions such as management, engineering, and various health fields require further education for continued certification or advancement, so a precedent for such recognition of effort already exists. Positive reinforcement of at-tendance at seminars and workshops would in turn encourage parti-cipation by those librarians who cannot afford the time or money to enroll in full–fledged courses. Who knows? Perhaps in the not-too– distant future we will all receive continuing education units at this Conference!

If library schools are involved in continuing education, part-icipation in such programs by faculty members must be regarded as one of their basic educational responsibilities. Involvement in providing continuing education is, after all, both a teaching func--tion and a service to the profession requiring significant prepara-tion and research time. Hence it should have a corresponding bear-ing on library school faculty tenure and promotion decisions.

Turning away from the continuing education of practitioners, let us look at a number of options that library schools have for integrating bibliographic instruction into the regular M.L.S. program. Notice we use the word program as opposed to curriculum, since the suggestions we offer include several broader alternatives.

One of the most easily arranged options would be for a library school to invite major BI figures from around the country to be convocation speakers or short--term in--residence faculty. Highlight--ing the importance of instruction in this way would at least intro--duce students to the various practical applications of the courses they are taking. Previously we stated that library schools could en--courage a sense of professionalism by supporting student attendance at library conferences. We would reiterate that recommendation as regards BI meetings. Attendance by students can serve both in lieu of BI content in the curriculum and, once BI is offered in some specific way, as a real--life complement to such content. We have in fact required the students currently enrolled in our L.S. 608 course to attend this Conference for at least one day since we feel there is no better exposure to the BI movement.

To begin the process of integrating bibliographic instruction into the library school curriculum, the first step for library educa--tors is to evaluate the existing offerings dealing with reference, bib--liography, administration, media and data processing, and special types of libraries. Those elements we have suggested which are missing from library education can then be plugged into each of these as appropriate, BUT, we would caution, this integration must be regular and systematic if it is to be effective, and all faculty mem--bers must agree on what components will be covered in what courses.

To move one step beyond integrating BI by bits and pieces into existing courses, a library school can create a whole biblio--graphic instruction module within a larger course, two or three weeks, for example, devoted to the basic principles of instruction. Preferably this module would be taught by someone with actual BI field experience who would work together with the regular faculty member to put BI in a practical and meaningful perspective.

Another closely--related option for library schools with more flexible academic calendars would be to offer a concentrated mini--course scheduled between two regular terms or during some other brief period. Again, we would point out the desirability of having such a mini--course team--taught by a faculty member and a librarian actually doing instruction. Since in both of these cases, module and mini--course, the time period involved is short, it should be feasible for a practicing librarian to leave a full--time job in order to teach BI intensively for a few days.

If students wish to explore one area of BI beyond a lecture in a regular course or a brief module or mini--course, an independent study program could be devised to center on search strategy, dis--cipline--oriented instruction, or any number of BI--related topics. Ideally such independent study would involve the student as an intern at an active BI program in the area so that the interaction of theory and practice could be observed first--hand. To extend the independent study idea even further, for those schools which still require a thesis, BI can be suggested as a significant research topic. Again a note of caution: before a library school goes beyond a basic introduction to BI, it is, of course, essential that the library science collection have the relevant support materials – journals, proceed-ings, monographs, and research reports – as well as that faculty be knowledgeable on the subject and its application.

So far we have suggested options which, singly or in com-bination, can provide a phasing of BI into the library school curri-culum until such time as a regular course can be offered. We feel very strongly that each library school should offer at least once per year a full course devoted to bibliographic instruction taught either by practitioners or by a practitioner--faculty team. This is not to say that BI need not be mentioned in other courses, far from it. Rather, the basic ideas of search strategy and the centrality of BI as a public service should still be re–stated throughout so that all library school students are exposed to these notions in some degree. Those students who then wish to delve into the topic more fully would have the opportunity to do so by electing the BI course, preferably in their last term, by which time they should have some sense of the rationale and content of BI. This is no more than is done now for other special topics such as collective bargaining in libraries, storytelling, or networking. At the University of Michigan, BI librarians are invited into general reference classes to introduce instruction as a public service, into bibliography classes to compare the discipline structures of social sciences and humanities fields, and into administration classes to discuss aspects of managing a BI program. Beyond this exposure, students can elect L.S. 608, a two–credit course offered in the spring (May–June) and which the three of us are currently team--teaching for the second year in a row.

Since BI is introduced in several other courses, you might won-der what it is that we include in L.S. 608. The truth is, we do not have any trouble at all filling twenty--eight contact hours, in fact, we have twice now had to compress or delete topics for which there was not time. Just yesterday we were describing L.S. 608 to some-one who commented, "Well, it sounds to me like you're trying a diagnostic approach to your BI class by filling in the gaps that exist in the rest of the curriculum." That is partly the case, but the course we have designed also tries to separate BI into its many com-ponents, examining each in some detail, then putting them in the context of a total BI program. As you can imagine from our pre-ceding remarks, we find it necessary to stress elements in L.S. 608 that we believe should rightly be taught elsewhere – a search strat-egy, question breakdown, and transactional analysis, to repeat a few – but we also try to provide the philosophical framework that underlies all of these elements in a bibliographic instruction program. Population and need determination, public relations, class prepara-- tion, lecture techniques, evaluation methods, long--range adminis- trative planning: these are all part of the course we teach. Neither a series of lectures scattered throughout the curriculum nor a brief module within another course can hope to offer the integration and perspective that a term--long course can provide.

It is not hard to create a list of topics; it is hard to squeeze them into a single term. As practitioners, once we had compiled a list of possible topics, we knew from experience that A needs to be covered before B which should precede C. Hindsight provides many advantages, and although we know we cannot hand our library students a BI prescription that will work at any institution where they are employed, there are common ideas and skills we can teach and common procedures we can share. Undoubtedly we are at-- tempting to teach the kind of course that we wish had been avail- able to us. Students should not have to learn suddenly that there is a slide--tape program they could have purchased, or that pre- paration of even a simple workbook requires hours of effort, or that there are other ways of doing instruction besides the one- hour lecture. The alternatives, the necessary elements, the problems that are bound to be encountered: these are lessons that library students should receive in school and then be able to apply and adapt to create a BI program, from scratch if necessary, tailored to a given institution's needs.

We have outlined several options which a library school can adopt to respond to the demand for librarians skilled in all aspects of bibliographic instruction. If we were given an ideal world and told we could choose any options, we would say, "All of them!" The more exposure students have to a concept, the better they will be able to apply it. Since no library school can afford to implement all of our suggestions, if we were forced to choose among them, we would heartily recommend a full--length course on BI taught regular- ly. We feel that only in a special course wholly devoted to BI can all of the forgotten factors be covered in context. We agree with the speaker yesterday who said that BI is as central to the func- tioning of a library as circulation, interlibrary loan, and acquisi- tions. BI is most definitely *not* a trend or an issue with the transi- tory significance those terms imply. By examining BI in detail as a permanent, central, and complex library function, students come to recognize and appreciate the relevance of their more theore- tical courses, sensing the influence of principles on practice.

One of the speakers today exhorted library school alumni to push for innovations in the curriculum based on the needs felt in the field. We would also exhort you to go beyond suggestions and become actively involved in teaching BI courses or segments of courses in library science. As BI practitioners you well understand and can well address the needs of library students for theoretical and practical information about instruction. You can provide them with unique insights, examples, and everyday working concerns that will make their subsequent teaching experiences far less traumatic than were your own first attempts. For us both individually and collectively, the highest compliment is to be told by our library school students that we have helped them "put it all together," meaning they are suddenly able to take all of the miscellaneous bits of information and training they have acquired and fit them into a coherent, creative whole, bibliographic instruction, that is as rewarding as it is challenging. If you do become so involved, we guarantee you will find yourself revising and improving your own instruction program to a degree you never thought possible. We have found that teaching about BI is a learning experience for ourselves as much as for our students, and, we trust, in the long run for future generations of college students as well.

We believe that for library school students and practicing librarians expecting to do instruction, the best background will always be the two–fold matrix of library education plus library experience. If once the right ingredients – many of which we have attempted to name – are mixed together and given a chance to react, the result will be dynamic, "new–breed" librarian--instructors who do not just placate users, but who, in fact, help educate them. The energy released in the process will quickly return to the system, invigorating and enriching the profession, the literature, library education, and -- not least of all -- the individual.

NOTES

1. Sue Galloway, "Nobody Is Teaching the Teachers," *Booklegger* 3 (Jan/Feb 1976): 29–31.

2. "Library Instruction: A Column of Opinion," *Journal of Academic Librarianship* 2 (Nov 1976): 240–41.

3. Benita J. Howell, Edward B. Reeves, and John van Willigen, "Fleeting Encounters -- A Role Analysis of Reference Librarian-Patron Interaction," *RQ* 16 (Winter 1976): 127.

LIBRARY ORIENTATION AND INSTRUCTION – 1976; AN ANNOTATED REVIEW OF THE LITERATURE

Hannelore B. Rader
Coordinator, Education and Psychology Division
Center of Educational Resources
Eastern Michigan University

This bibliography covers materials published during 1976, with some 1975 entries omitted from that year's listing. Citations from a number of foreign countries are included if published in English. A few items were not available for annotation. The growing interest in library use instruction is evident from the fact that the number of entries has doubled over those included in the bibliography for 1975.

Bailey, Martha J. "Bibliography and Reference Aids in the Physics Library." *Special Libraries,* 67 (April, 1976), pp. 202–207.
    This article discusses a variety of methods developed by the staff of the Purdue University Physics Library to help their patrons in using the library. Guides, handbooks, bibliographic lectures and other reference aids are some of the methods discussed here.

Beck, M.J. and D.L. Kuester. "Games for Goals." *Media Spectrum,* 3 (First Quarter, 1976), pp. 10–11.
    This brief article discusses the importance of games in teaching library skills to elementary level students. Several games are described.

Bibliographic Instruction Program. Kenosha, Wisconsin: University of Wisconsin–Parkside, 1976. 62p. ED 126 937
    This gives a description of the bibliographic instruction program at the University of Wisconsin–Parkside. The instructional objectives for the program are defined. Different phases of the program and evaluation procedures are described also.

Brewer, J.G. and P.J. Hills. "Evaluation of Reader Instruction." *Libri,* 26 (March, 1976), pp.55–66.
    This article tries to present the basic outline of the theory and methodology of evaluation of reader instruction and summarizes major references in this area. Some of the problems with the literature in this area have been that it evaluated orientation programs, highly sophisti-

---

*First published in Reference Services Review, v5n1, Jan.–Mar. 1977, pp.41-44.

cated teaching machines and not subject reader instruction. Also the evaluation of comparative studies of instruction is doubtful. Illuminative evaluation which has a humanistic rather than a scientific base could be a possible evaluative method in library instruction.

Brittain, Michael and Ann Irving. *Trends in the Education of Users of Libraries and Information Services in the USA.* A report submitted to the British Library Research and Development Department. Lough-borough University, April, 1976.
    This is a concise state–of–the–art review based on 80 inquiries and information from programs supported by the Council on Library Resources. A model of a typical library instruction program and an index are included.

Chapman, Geoffrey. *Prospective Manitoba Teachers and the Library.* Ottawa, Canada: Canadian Library Association, 1975. Occasional Paper No. 84.
    This work discusses the lack of library use instruction from elementary through higher education. The author points out the importance of library use instruction to prospective teachers. Education students at the University of Manitoba were tested on their library skills knowledge and found sadly lacking in this area. It is advocated that teachers and professors should be more library–oriented in their teaching.

Cooper, Noelle P. "Library Instruction at a University–Based Information Center: The Informative Interview." *R Q,* 15 (Spring, 1976), pp. 233–240.
    The article describes library instruction activities at Ohio State University where the Mechanized Information Center (MIC) (a computer-based literature search service) has provided opportunities for library instruction. Advantages and disadvantages of this type of library instruction are summarized.

Delaney, Jack J. "Teaching." *The Media Program in the Elementary and Middle School.* Hamden, Conn.: Linnet Books, 1976. pp. 83–96.
    This chapter talks about the school librarian as teacher of library use. The author discusses the role of principals and other teachers in this endeavor. Different types of library use instruction are explained and an outline for a "library lesson" is provided.

Douthwaite, M. "Learning Resource Center Orientation on Tape." *Previews,* 4 (May, 1976), p. 9.
    Nathan Hale High School in Seattle has a large Learning Resource Center. In order to help students become familiar with it a 15--minute tour on cassette has been developed. The tour is supplemented with printed information. Using this type of orientation has helped to solve the problems of large numbers of students. Students who missed

orientation and new students can take the tour any time.

"Draft Guidelines for Bibliographic Instruction in Academic Libraries."
College and Research Libraries News, 37 (December, 1976), p. 301.
    The guidelines for bibliographic instruction in academic libraries
were prepared by the ACRL Bibliographic Instruction. They were
adapted by the ACRL Board of Directors at the Midwinter meeting in
Washington, D.C.

Dunlap, Connie R. "Library Services to the Graduate Community: The
University of Michigan." *College and Research Libraries,* 37 (May, 1976),
pp. 247–251.
    This article describes unique problems and special needs of graduate
students and how one library attempts to provide specialized programs
to meet the needs of their graduate students. Also discussed are objectives, priority planning, staff involvement and the development of new
programs.

Duvall, Scott H. *Library Instruction: Two Teaching Methods.* Provo,
Utah: Brigham Young University, 1975. 52p. ED 112 898
    Two methods of instruction for the use of periodical, book and
newspaper indexes were compared -- the lecture and the self–study guide
method. The result showed no difference between the two methods.
The self–study guide is appended.

Farber, Evan I. and Thomas Kirk. "Instruction in Library Use." *The
ALA Yearbook.* Chicago, Ill.: American Library Association, 1976.
p. 59.
    This overview of library use instruction presents some of the signifi--
cant happenings in this area of librarianship during the 70's and points
out its most persistent problem -- systematic evaluation.

Fjallbrant, Nancy. "Teaching Methods for the Education of the Library
User." *Libri,* 26 (December, 1976), pp. 252–267.
    This article discusses objectives of library instruction, course con-
tent and timing of the instruction and various types of teaching methods.
The latter include lectures, seminars and tutorials, guided tours, audio-
visual instruction, printed guides, exercises, programmed instruction,
self–instruction and individualized instruction.

Foster, Barbara. "Hunter Midtown Library: The Closing of an Open
Door." *Journal of Academic Librarianship,* 2 (November, 1976), pp.
235–237.
    The author describes a library use instruction program for disadvan-
taged students at the Hunter College Midtown library from 1973 to
1976. The program proved quite successful but budget cuts forced its
elimination.

Galloway, Sue and Virginia Sherwood. "Essentials for an Academic Library's Instructional Service Program." *California Librarian,* 37 (April, 1976), pp. 44–49.

This article is based on a program presented on December 1, 1975 at the annual California Library Association Conference. Essential elements for an academic library instructional service program include administrative support, a program coordinator and office, a collection of curriculum materials and instructional librarians. Appended is a description for a library instruction coordinator.

Gebhard, Patricia. "How to Evaluate Library Instruction Programs." *California Librarian,* 37 (April, 1976), pp. 36–43.

This article defines evaluation as the systematic collection of information for comparison of terminal outcomes with stated objectives. Evaluation purposes are listed such as to determine a program's value and to improve instruction. Problems with evaluations are discussed. The article is based on a workshop on evaluation held in California in November, 1975 and the workshop participants concluded that they liked the use of both open and closed questions in library instruction evaluation. Sample evaluation forms are appended.

Gibson, Mary J. and Mildred Kaczmarek. *Finding Information in the Library: A Guide to Reference Sources for Rochelle High School Students.* Rochelle, Ill.: Rochelle Township High School, 1975. 74p. ED 114 117

The guide consists of a two–part handbook to introduce students to library sources in conjunction with their curriculum needs. The first part covers basic reference sources and library research skills, the second part covers subject–related reference sources.

Glogoff, S.J. and R.S. Seeds. "Interest among Librarians to Participate in Library–Related Instruction at the Pennsylvania State University Libraries." *Pennsylvania Library Association Bulletin,* 31 (May, 1976), pp. 55–56.

This gives the summary of a survey conducted in the Spring of 1975 to measure the interest among University Park and Commonwealth Campus Librarians of the Pennsylvania State University to participate in programs of course–related library instruction. The survey dealt with librarians' attitudes toward library–related instruction, their interest in participating in such instruction, their reason for not participating, specific subjects in which librarians would be willing to teach and their previous experiences. Due to the survey Penn State has identified a corps of librarians who could participate in a large scale library instruction program

Guide to the University of Kentucky Libraries. Lexington, Kentucky: University of Kentucky, 1976. 299p. ED 126 901

This is a collection of instructional materials for library use instruction developed as part of the College Library Program sponsored by the Council on Library Resources and the National Endowment for Humanities. (see also ED 126 900 for the second annual report of this program).

Hardesty, Larry. *Survey of the Use of Slide--Tape Presentations for Orientation and Instruction Purposes in Academic Libraries.* 1976. 183p. ED 116 711

This survey is based on responses from 88 academic libraries. It was found that few libraries have produced quality presentations and that the production of such presentations is time--consuming and expensive. For each responding library a summary of their slide--tape presentations is provided.

Hartley, A.A. "Hey That's Love Story." *North Carolina Libraries,* 34 (Spring, 1976), pp. 23--24.

At Appalachian State University librarians have developed programmed tapes for tours and such reference sources as *Readers' Guide, ERIC, Education Index, Monthly Catalog* and *New York Times Index.* These cassette tapes are available to patrons at any time and in portable format. Comments and opinions collected from patrons about these cassette programs are very positive.

Hickes, J.T. "Computer--Assisted Instruction in Library Orientation and Services." *Medical Library Association Bulletin,* 64 (April, 1976), pp. 238--40.

Hobbins, John. "Challenge to Teach: Instruction at Academic Libraries." *Argus,* 5 (May--August, 1976), p. 44.

Holley, Edward G. "Academic Libraries in 1876." *College and Research Libraries,* 37 (January, 1976), pp. 15--47.

The article points out that even a hundred years ago there was a certain amount of concern among academic librarians for better and more complete use of the collections. It was felt even then that librarians are educators and that the library should be the focal point of instruction on any campus.

Houston, S. "Atrisco Elementary, Albuquerque; Our Latest Project Is Attempting to Breathe Life into the Dewey Decimal System for Fifth Graders." *New Mexico Library Association Newsletter,* 4 (February, 1976), p. 3.

Iadanza, Margaret A. *The Development of a Bibliography of Library Skills Instructional Resources.* Mount Pleasant, Mi.: Central Michigan University, 1975. 72p. ED 114 085

This bibliography was compiled to familiarize librarians with method to assist library users in taking full advantage of library resources. Skills for using the libraries are dealt with in 1,000 entries by title, subject and media format.

Jeffries, J. "TV can Teach Readers Best." *Library Association Record,* 78 (April, 1976), p. 177.

Jones, A.M. and E.C. Theidling. "Reference Skills on Line; A Computer Assists Individually Planned Instruction." *Wisconsin Library Bulletin,* 72 (May, 1976), pp. 103–104.

Joyce, Beverly. "Library Instruction." *Oklahoma Librarian,* 26 (July, 1976), pp. 21–23.

This is a summary report on the Sixth Annual Conference on Library Orientation for Academic Libraries held at Eastern Michigan University, Ypsilanti on May 13 and 14, 1976.

Keene, M. and G.A. Waity. "Media Center Uses Games for Individual Learning and for Fun." *Wisconsin Library Bulletin,* 72 (May, 1976), pp. 101--102.

Keever, Ellen and James C. Raymond. "Integrated Library Instruction on the University Campus: Experiment at the University of Alabama." *Journal of Academic Librarianship,* 2 (September, 1976), pp. 185–187.

This is a report of an experimental program in library use instruc-- tion for English composition students at the University of Alabama, utilizing the Personalized System Instruction. Teaching assistants from the English Department and from the Graduate School of Library Science team teach in the freshman English course.

Kirkendall, Carolyn. "Library Instruction: A Column of Opinion." *Journal of Academic Librarianship,* 2 (September, 1976), pp. 188--189.

This column deals with the question whether or not library instruc-- tion should be an integrated and permanent component of an academic library's total service program. Two library administrators answer in the positive.

Kirkendall, Carolyn. "Library Instruction: A Column of Opinion." *Journal of Academic Librarianship,* 2 (November, 1976), pp. 240--241.

The column explores the question whether or not library schools agree on the need for library instruction in the library school curriculum.

Library school deans from the University of Michigan, University of Wisconsin--Madison, George Peabody College and Simmons College responded.

Koppelman, Connie. "Orientation and Instruction in Academic Libraries." *Special Libraries,* 67 (May--June, 1976), pp. 246–260.
  The author provides rationale for library orientation and instruction in academic libraries and proposes a variety of methods for such instruction. It is pointed out that faculty need as much orientation as students and such orientation can be utilized by the librarians to develop faculty cooperation for bibliographic instruction. Cooperative groups in library use instruction which can provide help to the beginning library instruction librarian are described.

Krier, Maureen. "Bibliographic Instruction: A Checklist of the Litera--ture, 1931--1975." *Reference Services Review,* 4 (January--March, 1976), pp. 7–31.
  This bibliography is arranged chronologically and author, subject and institution indexes are included. The list is not annotated but pro--vides descriptors for each entry.

Kusnerz, Peggy A. and Marie Miller. *Audio--Visual Techniques and Library Instruction.* Ann Arbor, Mi.: University of Michigan, 1975. 33p. ED 118 106
  This bibliography provides printed sources of information about the use of audio–visual materials with a view toward library instruction. Items included date from 1960--1975.

Library Games. Portland, Oregon: Portland Public Schools, 1976. 34p. ED 122 747
  This describes a collection of learning activities to reinforce library skills and to make the library a more attractive place for students.

Line, M.B. "Library--Based Information Services in Higher Education." Letters to the Editor. *Aslib Proceedings,* 28 (January, 1976), pp. 36--38.
  The author comments on Gerry Smith's article with the above title in *Aslib Proceedings,* 28 (1975), pp. 239--246. Various points are debated such as student motivation, importance of use instruction, com--puter searches and cost of services.

Lubans, John Jr. "Educating the Library User in England." *MPLA News--letter,* 20 (1975--76), p. 3.
  The article is based on a 1975 visit to the British Universities Sur--rey, Southampton, Bath, Loughborough, Leeds, Bradford, Lancaster and East Anglia. The author discusses briefly five areas of library use instruc--tion at these universities and compares them to U.S. activities: evalua--

tion, SCONUL slide--tape programs, integration of bibliographic instruc--
tion, universal library skills, freshman library skills.

Lubans, John Jr. *Program to Improve and Increase Student and Faculty
Involvement in Library Use.* Second Annual Progress Report to the
Council on Library Resources and the National Endowment for the
Humanities for the Year September 1, 1974--August 31, 1975. Boulder,
Colorado: University of Colorado, 1975. 38p. ED 114 097
    This report summarizes activities during the second year of the
CLR--NEH grant program to increase faculty involvement in library use
instruction in history and economics. A variety of evaluation instru--
ments were developed and are included.

Martinelli, James. "Bilingual Slide--Tape Library Orientation; An Un--
expected Frontier." *Audio Visual Instruction,* 21 (January, 1976), pp.
55--56.
    The article discusses library orientation on slide--tape for the Spanish
speaking students at Passaic County Community College in New Jersey.
The program covers the card catalog, encyclopedias, dictionaries, biograph
and periodical indexes in Spanish. The visuals are based on Chicano
interests.

Michalak, Thomas J. "Library Services to the Graduate Community: The
Role of the Subject Specialist Librarian." *College and Research Libraries,*
37 (May, 1976), pp. 257--265.
    This article discusses how direct contact between subject specialist
and user can provide dynamic information services. A subject specialist
can build an adequate collection, establish contact with user groups, give
library use instruction, provide current awareness and other bibliographi--
cal and reference services.

Midwest Federation of Library Associations. *Writing Objectives for
Bibliographic Instruction in Academic Libraries.* Kenosha, Wisconsin:
University of Wisconsin--Parkside, 1976.
    This work summarizes the workshops held during the meeting of the
Midwest Federation of Library Associations in Detroit, October 1--2,
1975. Included were sessions on developing good objectives, printed
instructional materials, audio--visual materials, lectures with transparen--
cies, exercises and separate courses in library use instruction.

Miller, S.W. *Library Use Instruction in Selected American Colleges.* MA
Thesis, University of Chicago, 1976. 91p.
    This dissertation describes the development of library use instruction
in the last fifteen years in American colleges and universities. Current
programs of library use instruction in 14 American colleges are discussed.
Course--related instruction seems to be prevalent but there seems to be
no consensus among librarians on the general principles of library use
instruction. Evaluation of these programs is a serious problem.

Painter, Ann. "A Guide to Better Student Use of Periodicals." *Catholic Library World,* 47 (April, 1976), pp. 380--382.

This article discusses student attitudes about periodicals, gives definitions of a serial and a periodical and points out the problems with the use of periodicals. It concludes by providing a six--step guide to periodical use.

Pollet, Dorothy. "New Direction in Library Signage: You Can Get There from Here." *Wilson Library Bulletin,* 50 (February, 1976), pp. 456--462.

This article discusses the problems with signage in libraries. In order to make libraries more accessible and understandable to users a variety of principles are necessary and these are specified here. Good signage will orient any patron and eliminate some of the repetitious information questions.

Quackenbusch, Roger E. "How to Use Biological Abstracts: An Exercise." *American Biology Teacher,* 38 (October, 1976), p. 431.

Describes a high school course on biological research which includes instruction on how to use *Biological Abstracts* followed by a practical application.

Rader, Hannelore B. *Faculty Involvement in Library Instruction.* Their Views on, Participation in, and Support of Academic Library Use Instruc--tion. Ann Arbor, Mi.: Pierian Press, 1976.

This is the sixth publication in the Library Orientation series and presents the papers from the Fifth Annual Conference on Library Orien--tation for Academic Libraries held at Eastern Michigan University, May 15--17, 1975. In addition to reporting on faculty involvement in library instruction programs at the University of Colorado, Earlham College, the University of Michigan, Eastern Michigan University and the State Uni--versity of New York at Syracuse, the publication summarizes also Project LOEX and some philosophies of library instruction.

Rader, Hannelore B. *Five--Year Library Outreach Orientation Program. Final Report.* Ypsilanti, MI.: Eastern Michigan University, 1975. 168p. ED 115 265

This is the final report of the five--year Library Outreach Orientation Program at Eastern Michigan University (1970--1975) sponsored by the Council on Library Resources and the National Endowment for the Humanities. Methodology, instructional materials, results and problems are summarized. Samples of the instructional materials are appended.

Rickwood, Peter C. "Introducing University Students to the Geological Literature." *Journal of Geological Education,* 23 (May, 1975), pp. 103--106.

This article deals with introducing students of geology to the litera--

ture in their field. Students involved are in third year geological courses at the University of New South Wales in Australia. The instruction is given by the course instructor and the Reader Education Librarian. This is followed by an assignment which involves exercises, described in the article.

Samuels, Marilyn S. "A Mini–Course in the Research Paper." *College English,* 38 (October, 1976), pp. 189–193.

This article describes the problem of the research paper in over-crowded freshman composition classes at City College, New York. A mini–course was planned to teach some students the methodology of the research paper. Once it was found that the course was working, it was converted into nine color videotapes of half-hour duration. The syllabus is included.

Schwartz, Edith and others. *Instruction Program for Library Media Centers.* Elkins Park, Pa.: Cheltenham Township School District, 1975. 49p. ED 114 082

The Cheltenham Township School District has compiled a guide for library instruction with learning objectives and activities for levels K-9 and a mini–course for grades 10–12. Course-related library instruction is emphasized. The entire library instruction plan is charted according to grade level and topics. Appended are a list of available lessons and a multi media bibliography.

Sim, Yong S. *An Individualized Library Orientation Program in Mercer County Community College Library: Curriculum Development.* 1975. 28p. ED 119 651

This describes a three-part 50-minute library orientation program for freshmen at Mercer County Community College in New Jersey. It includes a tour, information on the card catalog and on periodical indexes. Printed, audio and visual materials are utilized.

Smith, B.G. "How Do I Join Please? Initial Library Instruction in a Secondary School." *School Librarian,* 24 (June, 1976), pp. 109–111.

This article talks about library skill instruction in a British secondary school library. Three different approaches were utilized, talks to stu-dents, videotape instruction and slide–tape presentations. The uses, advantages and disadvantages of each method are described.

Stevenson, M.B. "Education in the Use of Information in University and Academic Environments." *Aslib Proceedings,* 28 (January, 1976), pp. 17–21.

This paper was presented at the 49th Aslib Annual Conference in Durham on September 22-25, 1975. It reviews library instruction activities from 1926 to present and assesses today's situation in Great Britain. The difference between orientation and bibliographic instruction is discussed. The importance of clearly defined objectives is stressed. It is suggested that academic staff with library qualifications and experience may be the best personnel to organize, prepare and carry out library use instruction.

Stoffle, Carla J. and others. *Library Instruction Programs, 1975; a Wisconsin Directory.* Madison, Wisconsin: Wisconsin Library Association, 1975. 201p. ED 118 157
    This directory summarizes library use instruction programs in Wisconsin academic, school and public libraries.

Taylor, T.K. "School Libraries and the Academic Progress of Students." *Australian Academic and Research Libraries,* 7 (June, 1976), pp. 117122.
    This article discusses the lack of library skills of students entering higher education in Australian institutions. Some of the blame is placed on the primary and secondary school librarians who are not teaching such skills. Better training for such librarians is proposed as well as more resources and supportive staff.

Tiffany, Constance J. and Philip J. Schwartz. "Need More Ready in Your Reference?KWOC It." *RQ,* 16 (Fall, 1976), pp. 3943.
    This article describes KWOC (keyword out of context) indexes and various self instructional packages developed by the librarians at the University of WisconsinStout. The KWOC indexes have been developed to help answer difficult and frequently asked reference questions, and they also provide individualized user instruction. An advantage of this index is the fact that it can be used any time the library is open and without reference librarians.

Toy, Beverly M. *Library Instruction at the University of California; Formal Courses.* Berkeley, California: University of California, 1975. 9p. ED 116 649
    This paper was presented at the Annual Meeting of the California Library Association in San Francisco, November 30December 3, 1975. It discusses the problems of establishing a formal library instruction program for undergraduates on the nine campuses of the University of California.

Trithart, David. *Library Resources in Education: An Introductory Module for Students and Teachers.* Potsdam, N.Y.: State University of New York, 1976. 32p. ED 124 129
    A selfinstruction module on basic library skills for students in education is presented as used in the library of SUNYPotsdam. Included are objectives, a tour, instructional activities for reference sources in education including ERIC and the curriculum materials center. Diagnostic self

instructional exercises and a self--test on basic library skills are also pro--
vided.

Tucker, Mark. *Five--Year Report and Evaluation on Project CLR No.
486 Presented to the Council on Library Resources.* Crawfordsville,
Indiana: Wabash College, 1976. 198p. ED 126 940
    This is a description of the five--year Library Instruction Project at
Wabash College sponsored by the Council of Library Resources and the
National Endowment for the Humanities. Appendices include the develop
instructional materials, evaluation instruments and other relevant infor--
mation.

Vernon, Christie. *An Individualized Program for Learning Resource
Center Orientation.* 1975. 66p. ED 114 086
    The Learning Resource Center at Thomas Nelson Community
College has developed a completely individualized, self--contained taped
orientation tour for the Center. The script and test questions are included.

Vernon, K.D.C. "Introducing Users to Sources of Information: The
Approach of the London Business School." *Aslib Proceedings,* 27
(November--December, 1975), pp. 468--473.
    This article describes library instruction provided by librarians
within a post--graduate business management course. An outline of the
library session is provided. Results of this endeavor have been positive for
all concerned and even the librarians found it to be an educational experi--
ence.

Ward, James E. "Library and Bibliographic Instruction in Southeastern
Academic Libraries." *Southeastern Librarian* (Fall, 1976), pp. 148--154.
    This article summarizes a survey of academic libraries in the
Southeast. Included were 608 questionnaires to ten states (Alabama,
Florida, Georgia, Kentucky, Mississippi, North Carolina, South Carolina,
Tennessee, Virginia and West Virginia). 337 returns are included in the
summary. Several recommendations are made to facilitate information
sharing between the libraries and toward the improvement of library
instruction programs. Appended are tables summarizing the data.

Werking, Richard H. *The Library and the College: Some Programs of
Library Instruction.* 1976. 32p. ED 127 917
    Noteworthy library instruction programs are described and library
instruction theories by Harvie Branscomb, Louis Shore, Patricia Knapp
and Evan Farber are discussed.

Whildin, Sara L. *A Directory of Library Instruction Programs in Penn--
sylvania Academic Libraries.* Pittsburgh: Pennsylvania Library Association, 1975. 37p. ED 118 071
    This directory summarizes library instruction programs in Pennsyl--

vania academic libraries based on 67 responses.

Whildin, Sara L. "Library Instruction in Pennsylvania Academic Libraries: A Survey Summary." *Pennsylvania Library Association Bulletin,* 31 (January, 1976), p. 8.

In May 1975 200 academic libraries in Pennsylvania were sent a questionnaire on library instruction in order to identify those libraries which were involved in library instruction, to assess their program content and to identify the persons involved in these programs. 67 responses were returned. The summary of these responses indicate that the state of library instruction in Pennsylvania resembles the state of library instruction nationwide. The results of the survey are also available in a form of a *Directory of Library Instruction Programs in Pennsylvania Academic Libraries* for $2.00 from PLA Headquarters.

Yaple, Henry M. *Programmed Instruction in Librarianship: A Classified Bibliography of Programmed Texts and Other Materials 1960–1974.* Urbana, Ill.: University of Illinois Graduate School of Library Science, 1976. Occasional Papers No. 124.

This bibliography identifies programmed materials for library education from 1960–1974. It contains programmed texts designed to instruct graduate students of librarianship as well as materials to teach various levels of students (elementary to higher education) about all aspects of the library. The entries are not annotated.

SEVENTH ANNUAL CONFERENCE ON LIBRARY ORIENTATION
FOR ACADEMIC LIBRARIES
May 12–13, 1977
EASTERN MICHIGAN UNIVERSITY

REGISTRANTS

Adams, Mignon
Lib. Instr. Unit
State College of New York
Oswego, NY 16126

Albright, Thomas E.
Ass't. Dir.
Michigan State Univ.
East Lansing, MI 48824

Amann, Cynthia
Ass't. Instr. Serv. Libr.
Univ. of Kentucky
Lexington, KY 40506

Baker, Jean S.
Ref. Libr.
Siena Heights College
Adrian, MI 49221

Beaubien, Anne
Ref. Libr., Grad. Lib.
Univ. of Michigan
Ann Arbor, MI 48109

Belanger, Mae D.
Serials Libr.
Ohio Dominican College
Columbus, OH 43219

Bell, Mary Beth
Inform. Serv. Libr.
Alderman Library
Univ. of Virginia
Charlottesville, VA 22901

Bennett, Joyce A.
Inst. Serv. Libr.

Sangamon State Univ.
Springfield, Ill 62704

Benson, Stanley H.
Lib. Dir.
Oklahoma Baptist Univ.
Shawnee, OK 74801

Boisse, Joe
Lib. Dir.
Univ. of Wisconsin–Parkside
Kenosha, WI 53140

Bremer, Paula
Ass't. Libr.
Univ. of Dubuque
Dubuque, Iowa 52001

Brown, Floy
Program Officer
NEH
Washington, DC 20506

Bunge, Charles A.
Dean Lib. School
Univ. of Wisconsin–Madison
Madison, WI 53706

Burke, Serena
Chairperson, Orient. Com.
Duke Univ. Library
Durham, NC 27706

Carter, Rubie T.
Ref. Libr., U.G. Lib.
Howard Univ.
Washington, DC 20001

Chadwick, Marietta
Engineering Ref. Libr.
Univ. of Toronto
Toronto, Ontario
Canada M5S 1A5

Childress, Cheryl
Pub. Serv. Libr.
Univ. of Virginia
Science/Technology
Charlottesville, VA 22901

Christopher, Virginia K.
Readers' Serv. Libr.
Elizabethtown College
Elizabethtown, PA 17022

Coblentz, John
Head Ref. Libr.
Appalachian State Univ.
Boone, NC 28608

Comes, James F.
Sci. Libr.
Ball State Univ.
Muncie, IN 47304

Covington, Paula Anne
Latin Amer. Studies Bibl.
Joint University Libraries
Nashville, TN 37203

Cragg, Carole
Ref. Libr.
Trinity College
Deerfield, IL 60015

Cravey, Pamela Austin
Bibl. Instr. Coord.
Georgia State Univ.
Atlanta, GA 30303

Delgado, Hannelore R.
Ed. & Psych. Coord.
Eastern Michigan Univ--CER

Ypsilanti, MI 48197

Dittman, Jeanne
Ass't. Libr.
Crumb Memorial Lib.
State Univ. Coll. at Potsdam
Potsdam, NY 13676

Dold, Jewell C.
Ref. Libr.
Northeastern Oklahoma State Univ.
Tahlequah, OK 74464

Douglas, Betty
Ass't. Ref. Libr.
Valdosta State College
Valdosta, GA 31601

Drury, Brother Wm. Francisco, CSC
Coord. Lib. Instr.
Univ. of Notre Dame
Notre Dame, IN 46556

Dudley, Mimi
Coord. Pub. & Instr. Serv.
UCLA College Library
Los Angeles, CA 90024

Durnell, Jane B.
Coord. Lib. Instr.
Univ. of Oregon
Eugene, OR 97403

Dusenbury, Carolyn
Instr. Libr.
Univ. of Utah–Marriott Lib.
Salt Lake City, UT 84102

Elliott, Bob
Lib. Instr. Libr.
Univ. of Windsor
Windsor, Ontario
Canada N9V 2P4

Espo, Hal

Library
Earlham College
Richmond, IN 47374

Eyler, Carol E.
Ass't. Libr.
Chatham College Lib.
Pittsburgh, PA 15232

Farber, Evan
Lib. Dir.
Earlham College
Richmond, Ind. 47374

Farmer, Ruth B.
Acquisition Libr.
Univ. of Central Arkansas
Conway, AR 72032

Flint, Elaine N.
Libr. -- Acquisitions
Glendale Comm. College
Glandale, AZ 85301

Flower, Kam
Ref. Dept.
Univ. of Maine
Orono, ME 04473

Freeman, Michael S.
Ass't. Chief Ref. Serv.
Dartmouth College
Hanover, NH 03755

Frost, William J.
Ref. Libr.
Bloomsburg State College
Bloomsburg, PA 17815

Gadsden, Alice H.
Ref. Libr.
Univ. North Carolina
Greensboro, NC 27412

Galligan, Sara

Ref. Libr.
Univ. of Michigan
Dearborn, MI 48128

George, Mary
Ref. Libr., Grad. Lib.
Univ. of Michigan
Ann Arbor, MI 48109

Gerity, Louise
LSEP Proj. Libr.
Lewis & Clark College
Portland, OR 97219

Gilbar, Richard
Ass't. Ref. Libr.
Univ. of Kansas
Lawrence, KS 66045

Girard, Martha
Info. Serv. Libr.
Johns Hopkins Univ.
Baltimore, MD 21218

Gwinn, Nancy E.
Info. & Pubs. Officer
Council on Lib. Resources
Washington, DC 20036

Hagle, Claudette
Instr. Gen. Ref. Dept.
Oklahoma State Univ.
Stillwater, OK 74074

Hahn, Doyne M.
Ref. Libr.
Ball State Univ.
Muncie, IN 47303

Halpern, Marilyn
Educ. Ref. Libr.
Bowling Green State Univ.
Bowling Green, OH 43403

Hammond, Nancy

Lib. Educ. Officer
Polytechnic of No. London
London, ENG N78DB

Hardesty, Larry
Head of Ref. Dept.
DePauw Univ.
Greencastle, IN 46135

Harrison, James O., Jr.
Circulation Libr.
Georgia Southern College
Statesboro, GA 30458

Haskell, Peter
CLR Intern
Indiana Univ.
Bloomington, IN 47401

Havener, W. Michael
Ass't. Ref. Libr.
Univ. of South Carolina
Columbia, SC 29201

Hawbaker, A. Craig
Act. Dir. of User Serv. &
Library Learning Prog.
Kearney State College
Kearney, NE 68847

Heidler, Robert S.
Ref. Libr. & Chm. Instr. Com.
Bowling Green Univ.
Bowling Green, OH 43403

Herndon, Gail A.
Ref. Libr.
Ohio State Univ.
Columbus, OH 43201

Hickey, Damon D.
Ass't. Lib. Dir. Pub. Serv.
Guilford College
Greensboro, NC 27410

Hill, Mabel
Libr. -- Cataloger
Jackson Community College
Jackson, MI 49201

Hinkley, Louise
Library
Earlham College
Richmond, IN 47374

Hinz, Joan
Ref. Libr.
Kalamazoo College
Kalamazoo, MI 49007

Hitt, Charles J.
Coord. Instr. Serv.
Mankato State Univ.
Mankato, MN 56001

Hogan, Sharon
Ref. Libr., Grad. Lib.
Univ. of Michigan
Ann Arbor, MI 48109

Hooper, James Edward
Dir. Lib. Serv.
Young Harris College
Young Harris, GA 30582

Hubbard, Terry E.
Instr. Coord.
Univ. of Alaska
Fairbanks, AK 99701

Hudson, Phyllis J.
Ref. Lib.
Florida Technical Univ.
Orlando, FL 32816

Humphrey, Ellen G.
Humanities Libr.
Univ. of Calgary
Calgary, Alberta
Canada T2N 1N4

Johnson, Gladys Marie
Ass't. Libr.
Jackson State Univ.
Jackson, MS 39213

Johnson, Kathy
Ass't. Humanities Libr.
Univ. of Nebraska
Love Library
Lincoln, NE 68588

Johnson, O. Clayton
Ass't. Chancellor
Univ. of Wisconsin--Parksode
Kenosha, WI 53140

Jonas, Eva S.
Ref. Libr.
Harvard Univ.
Cambridge, MA 02138

Keever, Ellen H.
Readers' Serv. Libr.
The College of Wooster
Wooster, OH 44691

Keller, Nancy J.
Ref. Libr.
Ohio State Univ.
Columbus, OH 43214

Kennedy, Jim
Library
Earlham College
Richmond, IN 47374

Kirk, Tom
Library
Earlham College
Richmond, IN 47374

Kirkendall, Carolyn
Dir.--Proj. LOEX
Eastern Mich. Univ. -- CER
Ypsilanti, MI 48197

Krompart, Janet
Assoc. Dean Tech. Serv.
Oakland Univ.
Rochester, MI 48063

Kuhtz, Mary Lee
History Libr. Ref. Dept.
Bowling Green State Univ.
Bowling Green, OH 43402

Kupersmith, John
Ref. Libr.
Univ. of Pennsylvania
Philadelphia, PA 19104

Larson, Julie
Curric. Libr.
Univ. of Wisconsin
Milwaukee, WI 53211

Lee, Flossy T.
Head. Ref. Dept.
State Univ. of New York
Binghamton, NY 13901

Lee, Leon
Teacher of English
Young Harris College
Young Harris, GA 30582

Lichtenberg, Rita
Ref. Libr. U.G. Lib.
Indiana Univ.
Bloomington, IN 47401

deLoach, Lucy
Ref. Libr.
Univ. of Hawaii
Honolulu, HA 96822

Maltese, Susan
Coord. Lib. Serv.
Oakton Community College
Morton Grove, IL 60053

Manley, Nancy Hill
Ass't. U.G. Libr.
Univ. of ILlinois
Urbana, IL 61801

Marshall, A.P.
Ref. Libr.
Eastern Mich. Univ. – CER
Ypsilanti, MI 48197

Maughan, Laurel S.
Proj. Libr. LSEP
Oregon State Univ.
Corvallis, OR 97331

McCargar, Susan
Libr. Spec. Serv. Div.
Yankee Book Peddler, Inc.
Ypsilanti, MI 48197

McCord, S. Joe
Ass't. Dir. Pub. Serv.
Univ. Texas Health Sci. Cen.
Dallas, TX 75235

McFeely, Mary Drake
Ref. Libr.
Smith College
Northampton, MA 01063

McGrew, Mary Lou
Ass't. Prof. Dept. Lib. Sci.
Univ. of Northern Iowa
Cedar Falls, IA 50613

McNeill, Joseph P., Jr.
Tech. Serv. Libr.
Austin College
Sherman, TX 75090

McVey, Susan C.
Ref. Libr.
Oklahoma City Univ.
Oklahoma City, OK 73106

Meckstroth, Patricia Ann
Gen. College Libr.
Milner Library
Illinois State Univ.
Normal, IL 61761

Mertins, Barbara
Ass't. Prof.
West Virginia Univ.
Morgantown, WV 26506

Mielke, John
Act. Head, Ref. Serv. Dept.
State Univ. of New York
Albany, NY 12222

Miller, Constance
Pub. Serv. Libr.
St. John's Univ.
Collegeville, MN 56321

Millson--Martula, Christopher
Dir. Lib.
St. Xavier College
Chicago, Il 60655

Minock, Mary F.
Ref. Lib. Instr.
Lansing Community College
Lansing, MI 48823

Moe, Claudia
Sr. Ref. Libr.
West Virginia Univ.
Morgantown, WV 26506

Myers, Susan L.
Sr. Ref. Libr.
Tutt Library
The Colorado College
Colorado Springs, CO 80903

Nagpal, Regina
Ref. Ass't.
Wittenberg Univ.

Springfield, OH 45501

Nelson, Ilene
Proj. Lib. CLR Lib. Serv.
Univ. of South Carolina
Aiken, SC 29801

Nelson, Margaret R.
Ref. Libr.
Ball State Univ.
Muncie, IN 47304

Newkirk, Leone I.
Prog. Assoc.
Council on Lib. Resources
Suite 620, One Dupont Circle
Washington, DC 20010

Nielsen, Carol S.
Lib. Sci. Libr.
Univ. of North Carolina
Chapel Hill, NC 27514

Nitschke, Eric R.
Ref. Libr.
Emory Univ.
Atlanta, GA 30322

Nixon, Judith
Ref. Libr.
Univ. of Wisconsin
Platteville, WI 53818

Ormondroyd, Joan L.
Proj. Libr.
Cornell Univ.
Ithaca, NY 14853

Pearson, Lennart
Dirl Lib.
Presbyterian College
Clinton, SC 29325

Pillepich, Mary
Lib. Sci. Libr.

Univ. of Illinois
Urbana, IL 61801

Polit, Rebecca
Ass't. Libr. Ref. & Lib. Instr.
Indiana Univ.
Bloomington, IN 47401

Kathleen A. Powers
Ref. Libr.
Boston College
Bapst Library
Chestnut Hill, MA 02167

Pressau, Jane T.
Student Serv. Libr.
Presbyterian College
Clinton, SC 29325

Pritchard, Hugh
Ref. Libr.
Univ. of New Hampshire
Durham, NH 03824

Pyrch, Jeannette
Ref. Libr.
Sedgewick Library
Univ. of British Columbia
Vancouver, British Columbia
Canada V6T 1W4

Reichel, Mary
Sr. Ref. Libr. U.G. Lib.
State Univ. of New York
Buffalo, NY 14214

Rigg, Sarah L.
Pub. Serv. Libr.
West Georgia College
Carrollton, GA 30177

Roach, Jeannetta
Head Libr.
Tougaloo College
Tougaloo, MS 39174

Rodgers, Sharon
Soc. Sci. Subj. Spec.
Univ. of Toledo
Toledo, OH 43606

Roehling, Steve
Ass't. Libr.
Emory & Henry College
Emory, VA 24327

Rottsolk, Katherine M.
Library
St. Olaf College
Northfield, MN 55057

Ruskell, Virginia
Ass't. Ref. Libr.
West Georgia College
Carrollton, GA 30117

Schlauch, Edward
Ref. Libr.
Sigmund Samuel Lib.
Univ. of Toronto
Toronto, Ontario
Canada M5S 1A5

Schobert, Timothy
Orient. Libr.
Univ. of Ottawa
Ottawa, Ontario
Canada K1N 6N5

Schwartz, Barbara
Ref. Libr.
Zahn IMC -- Temple Univ.
Philadelphia, PA 19122

Sharma, Prabha
Instr. Bibl./Subj. Spec.
Univ. of Alabama
Huntsville, AL 35807

Sherrill, Rebecca L.
Ass't. Libr. Pub. Serv.

Miami Univ.
Hamilton, OH 45013

Shoichet, Mary E.
Libr. I, Sci. Lib.
Wayne State Univ.
Detroit, MI 48202

Simon, Rose
Library–Faculty Liaison
Guilford College
Greensboro, NC 27410

Smith, Fred E.
Prof. Ref. Lib.
Shippensburg State College
Shippensburg, PA 17201

Soczka, Jan
Ref. Libr.
Univ. of Wisconsin
Milwaukee, WI 53201

Sparks, Rita
Ref. Libr.
Oakland Univ.
Rochester, MI 48063

Spicer, Caroline T.
Head Ref. Grad. Lib.
Cornell Univ.
Ithaca, NY 14853

Stanton, Vida C.
Ass't. Prof. Sch. Lib. Sci.
Univ. of Wisconsin
Milwaukee, WI 53201

Stevenson, Marsha
Ref. Libr.
Ohio State Univ.
Newark, OH 43055

Stinson, Patricia A.
Ref. Libr. Soc. Sci.

Texas Tech Univ.
Lubbock, TX 79404

Stoffle, Carla J.
Asst. Dir., Lib.
Univ. of Wisconsin -- Parkside
Kenosha, WI 53140

Surprenant, Thomas T.
Teach. Ass't.
Univ. of Wisconsin
Madison, WI 53706

Tiefel, Virginia
Assoc. Head Libr.
Hiram College
Hiram, OH 44234

Tolliver, Nellie W.
Ref. Libr.
Jackson State Univ.
Jackson, MS 39217

Treadway, Cleo
Dir. Libr. Serv.
Tusculum College
Greenville, TN 37743

Trithart, David
Curric. Materials Libr.
State University College
Potsdam, NY 13676

Tynan, Elizabeth
Ass't. Ref. Libr.
Denison Univ.
Granville, OH 43023

Tyson, John C.
Ref. Libr.
West Virginai Univ.
Morgantown, WV 26506

Ubbelohde, Susan
Library
Earlham College
Richmond, IN 47374

VanEss, James E.
Ref. Libr.
Carroll College
Waukesha, WI 53186

Vaughan, James M.
Ass't. Libr.
Elmhurst College
A.C. Buehler Lib.
Elmhurst, IL 60126

Violette, Judith
Head, Ref. Dept.
Indiana Univ.–Purdue Univ.
Fort Wayne, IN 46305

Ward, James E.
Dir. of the Lib.
David Lipscomb Colleg
Nashville, TN 37203

Weddle, Karen S.
Ref. Serv. Coord.
Univ. of Oklahoma
Norman, OK 73019

Weis, Aimee L.
Ref. Libr.
Community College of Philadelphia
Philadelphia, PA 19107

Werking, Richard
Project Libr.
Lawrence Univ.
Appleton, WI

White, Anita I.
Ass't. Libr.
Community College of Allegheny Co.
Pittsburgh, PA 15212

Wiggins, Marvin E.
Gen. Ref. Libr.
Brigham Young Univ.
Provo, UT 84601

Williams, Mitsuko
Ass't. Biol. Libr.
Univ. of Illinois
Urbana, IL 61801

Wilson, R.G.
Head, Pub. Serv.
Southern Alberta Inst. of Tech.
Calgary, Alberta
Canada T2M 0L4

Yee, Sandra
Ref. Libr.
Muskegon Community College
Muskegon, MI 49442

Young, Alene
Library
North Carolina A&T State Univ.
Greensboro, NC 27411

Young, Tommie M.
Dir. Lib. Serv.
North Carolina A&T State Univ.
Greensboro, NC 27411